W9-ANQ-793

CONTENTS

By matching up the guides at the edge of this page with the marks opposite them along the edge of the book, you can quickly turn to the unit containing the material you want.

K44

REFERENCE MANUAL

FOR OFFICE PERSONNEL

5th EDITION

Clifford R. House
President, Cincinnati Technical Institute
and
Apollonia M. Koebele

SOUTH-WESTERN PUBLISHING CO.

Cincinnati, OH 45227 • Chicago, IL 60644 • Dallas, TX 75229

New Rochelle, NY 10802 • Burlingame, CA 94010

COPYRIGHT © 1970
by
SOUTH-WESTERN PUBLISHING CO.
Cincinnati, Ohio

All Rights Reserved

The text of this publication, or any part thereof,
may not be reproduced or transmitted in any
form or by any means, electronic or mechanical,
including photocopying, recording, storage in an
information retrieval system, or otherwise, without the prior written permission of the publisher.

Library of Congress Catalog Card Number: 68-9795

12 13 H 9 8

Printed in U.S.A.

Preface

Reference Manual for Office Personnel, Fifth Edition, is designed to serve as a supplementary textbook in the education of office personnel and as a handy reference for those engaged in office work. This Fifth Edition incorporates the best features of the previous editions (entitled *Reference Manual for Office Employees*). Material drawn from previous editions has been updated and supplemented with new material.

The content of the Manual is divided into twenty-one units of related information and guides. Boldface headings, as well as an efficient numbering system, guide the student or office worker quickly to specific items of information within the units. A comprehensive, liberally cross-referenced index further increases the user's access to needed information. In addition, the Table of Contents has been reproduced on both the front and back flyleaves. By aligning the guides on the flyleaves with the marks opposite them at the edge of the manual pages, the user can quickly locate the unit that contains the material he wants.

To increase the usefulness and enhance the value of the Manual, the following major improvements have been made:

1. In Unit 1, the suggestions on typewriter maintenance have been revised to conform to the latest recommendations of typewriter manufacturers. In addition, instructions for typing offset masters have been added.

2. Two letter placement tables are now included in Unit 4: (1) floating dateline placement, now most commonly used in business; (2) fixed dateline placement, until recently the method most often taught in high schools and colleges.

3. Unit 6 now contains a quick-reference nonmathematical method of planning tabulations.

4. In Unit 8, explicit instructions for spacing with each mark of punctuation are given.

5. The spelling aids in Unit 10 have been strengthened by expanding the lists of illustrative words that accompany them.

6. The guides for word division in Unit 12 have been made to harmonize with *Word Division Manual,* Second Edition, by Silverthorn and Perry—a manual based upon the merging of two independent word studies of approximately 300,000 words each.

7. Unit 14 on "Abbreviations" has been greatly expanded. A section on data processing abbreviations has been added. In addition, a

list of the two-letter state, district, and territory ZIP Code abbreviations is included. Current abbreviations for Canadian provinces are also listed.

8. The postal information presented in Unit 15 was submitted to and approved by the Post Office Department.

9. Similarly, the information on telegrams in Unit 17 was updated and approved by Western Union. Illustrations include a Telefax message and a file copy of a message telephoned to the Western Union office.

10. Some suggestions on conducting and reporting informal business meetings have been added to Unit 18.

11. Outlines are now included in the unit on manuscript preparation. Furthermore, the guides on typing footnotes and bibliographical items have been revised to agree with the consensus of authoritative handbooks, insofar as consensus exists.

It is important to point out that recognized authorities do not always agree on matters of style, on preferences in grammatical usage, on the sequential elements of footnotes, and other stylistic features of written communication. When consensus among such authorities does exist, it is reflected in this Manual. When, however, different authorities indicate different preferences, this Manual represents what seems to be majority opinion; and in many instances it indicates that more than one treatment is acceptable.

Many of the foregoing improvements, as well as others not mentioned specifically, were made at the suggestion of teachers of business and communication subjects. To these users of preceding editions, we are especially grateful. In addition, grateful acknowledgment is extended to the Cincinnati and Suburban Bell Telephone Company, the American Telephone and Telegraph Company, the Cincinnati Legal Secretaries Association, the Ohio Association of Legal Secretaries, the United States Post Office, and the Western Union Telegraph Company. All these contributed substantially to make this an up-to-date, useful Manual for office personnel and those who are preparing to become office workers.

CLIFFORD R. HOUSE

APOLLONIA M. KOEBELE

Table of Contents

Tips on Typing

Dust, dirt, and grit are major causes of typewriter malfunctions. Even if a dirty typewriter continues to function, its action becomes sluggish and erratic.

Typewriter erasers contain a gritty abrasive used to grind away the top surface of the paper as the rubber removes the ink. If eraser crumbs fall into the type-bar mechanism, key action becomes sluggish, the abrasive causes the machine to wear at an accelerated rate, and the type bars begin to stick and jam.

Speed alone does not make one an expert typist. The real professional is careful about style and placement of materials and always produces a sharp, clear, clean impression on originals, carbons, and duplicated copies.

1-1. Contents of a Cleaning Kit

1. A long-handled brush for dusting inside the machine
2. A short, stiff-bristled brush for cleaning type
3. Platen (cylinder) cleaner and type cleaner
4. Cheesecloth for dusting the machine

1-2. Cleaning the Typewriter

1. Dust the typewriter daily. Use the long-handled brush to remove dust and dirt from places not accessible with a cloth.
2. Clean the carriage rails with a cloth or a brush by moving the carriage to the extreme left and then to the extreme right.
3. Clean the type daily with a cloth or dry brush. Once weekly use a brush and cleaning fluid. After brushing the type faces with cleaning fluid, remove excess cleaning fluid and dirt with cheesecloth.
4. Some typists prefer to clean the type by following these steps:

    a. Insert a sheet of absorbent paper into the typewriter.
    b. Set the ribbon control for stencil typing.
    c. Daub the type faces with type cleaner.
    d. Strike each key several times so that dirt loosened by the type cleaner may be deposited on the absorbent paper.

1-3. Oiling the Typewriter

You may oil the carriage rails sparingly if they are first cleaned thoroughly. Oiling any other part of the typewriter is a job for qualified service personnel. Never attempt to oil any part of the type-bar mechanism. Sticking type bars are the result of dust, eraser grit, or accumulated gum—not lack of lubrication.

1-4. Erasing Errors

1. Lift the paper bail. If the error is on the upper two thirds of the page, turn the platen forward. If the erasure is to be made in the lower third of the paper, turn the platen backward so the paper will not slip out of the typewriter while the correction is being made.
2. Move the carriage to the extreme right or left so the eraser crumbs will not fall into the type basket.
3. Place a blotter, stiff card, metal guard, or plastic shield between the original sheet and the dull side of the carbon.
4. Erase the error carefully. Too much pressure on the eraser may cause a tear.
5. Be careful not to smear material adjacent to the error. A pointed eraser and/or an erasing shield act as a preventative.
6. Use a clean typewriter eraser of the type that is most satisfactory for the grade of paper being used.
    a. Bond paper requires a hard eraser.
    b. Less expensive grades of paper and carbon copies require a softer eraser.
    c. A razor blade is useful for erasing on bond paper and when making a slight correction.
7. Blow or brush the eraser crumbs away from the typewriter as well as from the copy.
8. Shift the blotter or card in front of the second carbon if more than one copy is being made. Erase the error. Again blow or brush the eraser crumbs away. Follow this procedure for succeeding carbon copies.
9. Type the correction with a light touch. With a little care, the corrected area can be made to match the surrounding characters.

1-5. Squeezing and Spreading Letters

1. **Squeezing Within a Word.** To squeeze an additional letter into a word typed incorrectly on a standard typewriter—
    a. Erase the incorrect word.
    b. Position the carriage at the space after the last letter of the preceding word.
    c. Press down and hold the space bar; strike the first letter of the word.
    d. Release the space bar; then press it down again and hold it; strike the next letter.
    e. Continue in this manner for each remaining letter and the word will be squeezed into the space.
    f. If the space bar does not half-space, partially depress the backspace key to half-space.

2. **Squeezing at the Beginning of a Word.** To squeeze an omitted letter at the beginning of a word—

a. Position the carriage at the space after the last letter of the preceding word.
b. Press down and hold the space bar; then strike the omitted letter.

3. Squeezing at the End of a Word. To squeeze an omitted letter at the end of a word—

a. Position the carriage at the space after the last letter of the word.
b. Press down halfway and hold the backspace key; strike the omitted letter.

4. Spreading a Word—Manual Typewriter. To spread the letters of a word on a standard typewriter—

a. Erase the incorrect word.
b. Position the carriage as if you were going to type the first letter of the incorrect word in its regular position following the space.
c. Press down and hold the space bar; strike the first letter of the word.
d. Release the space bar; then repeat the process for each of the remaining letters.
e. If the space bar does not half-space, partially depress the backspace key to half-space.

5. Spreading a Word—Electric Typewriter. To spread or squeeze words typed incorrectly on an electric typewriter—

a. Move the carriage backward a half space by pushing the carriage back the half space with your hand; move the carriage forward the half space by holding the carriage with your hand and allowing it to move forward a half space as you touch the space bar.
b. Type the corrections on the half spaces.

1-6. Typing a Letter with Multiple Carbon Copies

1. Be sure to make at least one carbon copy as an office record for the files.
2. Show all corrections and erasures on the carbon copy as well as on the original. The carbon copy must be an exact duplicate of the original. File copies should appear as neat as the original regardless of the quality of paper used.
3. Use the weight and finish of carbon paper that is suitable for the type of work. Select a carbon paper according to the weight and quality of the stationery, the number of copies required, the size of the type—pica or elite—and the particular touch of the operator. The durability of carbon paper depends upon its finish. Carbon paper may be soft, medium soft, medium, medium hard, or hard; and its weight may be light, medium, or standard.

1-a. Assembling a Carbon Pack

1-b. Inserting the Carbon Pack

    a. A typist with an average touch usually gets better results by using medium finish carbon with pica type and medium hard with elite type.

    b. A typist with a heavy touch requires a medium hard finish for pica type and a hard finish for elite type.

4. Check to see that the glossy sides of the carbon sheets face the same way. The glossy sides should be facing you when the sheets are inserted in the typewriter. When the sheets are in the machine ready for typing, the glossy surface will be turned away from you.

5. Handle carbon paper carefully since careless handling or wrinkled carbon paper causes smudgy copies and "trees" on the duplicates. Worn-out carbon paper should be discarded.

6. When typing a letter with multiple carbon copies, it is necessary to assemble the carbon pack quickly and efficiently. Three methods of assembling carbon packs are commonly used: (1) the desk assembly method, (2) the machine assembly method, and (3) the slotted desk drawer assembly method.

7. In the desk assembly method of assembling a carbon pack, follow these steps:

    a. Place a sheet of paper for a carbon copy (second sheet) on the desk; on top of that sheet place a sheet of carbon paper, *glossy side down.* Add one set (a second sheet and a carbon) for each extra copy desired. Place the letterhead or a plain sheet of heavier paper on top of the pack for the original copy.

    b. Turn the pack around so the glossy sides of the carbon sheets face you.

    c. Straighten the pack by tapping the sheets gently on the desk.

    d. Insert the pack by holding it firmly in one hand while turning the platen slowly with the other.

8. To insert the carbon pack into the typewriter and to get it started easily—

**1-c. Assembling a
Carbon Pack in a
Typewriter**

**1-d. Removing the
Carbon Sheets**

   a. Release the paper-release lever.
   b. Start the pack into the typewriter.
   c. Reset the paper-release lever.
   d. Feed the pack into the machine.
   e. To keep the sheets straight when feeding, place the carbon pack under the flap of an envelope or in the fold of a plain sheet of paper. After the pack has been inserted, remove the envelope or paper fold.
   f. To avoid wrinkling, release and reset the paper-release lever after the pack has been inserted.

9. In the machine assembly method of assembling a carbon pack, follow these steps:

   a. Arrange a stack of white sheets (with the original on top) for insertion into the typewriter.
   b. Insert the sheets until the tops are gripped slightly by the feed rolls; then lay all but the last sheet over the top of the machine.
   c. Place carbon sheets between the sheets of paper with the glossy sides toward you. Flip each sheet back as you add each carbon.
   d. Roll the pack into typing position.
   e. After the typing is completed, remove the carbon sheets. As the carbon sheets do not extend to the top edge of the paper, it is easy to remove all the sheets at one time by pulling them out as you hold the left top edge of the paper.

10. In the slotted desk drawer assembly method of assembling a carbon pack, the secretary utilizes the arrangement of the stationery supplies in a slotted desk drawer. The letterheads should be kept in the slot at the extreme left; the carbon sheets should be kept in the next slot to the right; the second sheets should be kept in the third slot. With this arrangement, follow these steps:

   a. Pick up a letterhead with your left hand and a sheet of carbon paper with your right hand. Pull the sheets slightly forward;

then grasp both sheets with your left hand as you reach with your right hand to pull the second sheet into position.

b. Pull the sheets from the slots.

c. Straighten the pack by tapping it gently on the desk as you hold the sides of the sheets loosely by both hands.

d. Add a second sheet and a carbon for any additional copies that you need.

e. Insert the pack into the typewriter in the usual manner.

1-7. Other Methods of Typing Multiple Copies

1. **Photocopying.** Stationers have designed and patented several short-cuts that allow for complete file records with a minimum of effort. One of these calls for the installation of duplicating devices that reproduce complete letters similar to photostatic copies. In lieu of dictating a reply to the letter, the recipient makes comments by hand or on the typewriter in the margin of the incoming piece of mail. The letter is then reproduced, and the copy is forwarded to the sender. The original letter, properly annotated, is placed in the company file.

2. **Business-Reply Messages.** A business-reply message is a two-way, within-company communication that provides space for a reply on the same page as the original message. (See page 7.)

   a. The sender types the message in the column at the left, keeps the second copy (yellow), and forwards the other two copies (white and pink) to the addressee.

   b. The addressee types the reply in the column at the right, keeps the third copy (pink), and returns the original copy (white) to the sender.

1-8. Stenciling

1. Prepare a typewritten model copy. Make sure that the copy is placed on the page so that it will be within the stencil guide marks.
2. Clean the typewriter type (as directed on page 1).
3. Adjust the ribbon-control lever to stencil position.
4. Place the porous cushion sheet between the stencil sheet and the backing sheet. This porous cushion prevents letter cutout.
5. Place the top edge of the model copy at the corner marks of the stencil to determine the placement of the first line of copy. Use the printed numbers on the stencil to guide you.
6. Insert the stencil pack, which includes the backing sheet, the cushion, and the stencil sheet, into the machine with the backing sheet next to the platen.
7. Type the stencil, using a uniform, staccato typing stroke.
8. Proofread the stencil before removing it from the typewriter. If you made any errors, correct them with correction fluid.

SAM-CAP COMPANY	

REPLY-O-GRAM

SAM-CAP COMPANY
400 Indian Avenue, East
Philadelphia, PA 19134

MESSAGE	REPLY
TO ⌐ Frederick Schlimm 　Production Manager　　　　　┐ 　L　　　　　　　　　　　　　┘ DATE September 15, 19--	DATE September 20, 19-- 　　　Please revise our Order #427 as follows: 　　　Item 7:　5 concrete mixers, 　　　　　　　　Model CC 4.5, at 　　　　　　　　$187.50 each

MESSAGE:

　　The 5½ cu. ft. concrete mixer Model CC 5.5 is no longer manufactured. Perhaps the mixer Model CC 4.5, which is described on page 347 of the Acme catalog, will be satisfactory, even though it has a slightly smaller capacity. If so, we shall order it for you.

　　Please let us know if you wish the Model CC 4.5 ordered.

BY　　John Thompson, Purchasing Agent

SIGNED　Frederick Schlimm

1-e. Business-Reply Message

a. Smooth the surface of the error with a burnisher to close perforations in the stencil.

b. Place a pencil between the stencil and the cushion sheet.

c. Apply a thin coating of correction fluid over the error.

d. Allow the correction fluid to dry before retyping—approximately 20 to 30 seconds for a standard typewriter and 2 to 3 minutes for an electric typewriter. On a manual typewriter, use a light stroke in typing the correction; on an electric typewriter, set the impression control for a light impression.

9. When rolling the platen, hold all sheets firmly together to avoid wrinkling the stencil.

1-9. Preparing a Master for Spirit Duplication (Hectograph)

1. Prepare a typewritten model copy.

2. Clean the typewriter type (as directed on page 1.)

3. Procure a sheet of master paper (a special coated paper) and a sheet of special carbon (duplicator) paper. Some typists use a sheet of heavy paper for a backing sheet. The glossy side of the carbon should face you as you type so that the carbon appears in reverse on the back of the master sheet.

4. Prepared "sets" may be obtained from office supply companies. Before inserting a set, remove the protection sheet found between the master sheet and the carbon.

5. Type with a firm, even stroke on a manual typewriter. Set the control adjustment for a lower impression on an electric typewriter.

6. Avoid making errors; but if a correction is necessary, use one of three methods. (You need not erase the front of the master sheet.)

   a. Use a soft eraser to rub out the error on the reverse side of the master sheet. The slight smudge that appears will not reproduce when copies are run. Next, cut off an unused corner of the carbon and place it (facing the error) between the carbon sheet and the master sheet. Then type the correction. Remove the piece of carbon before proceeding with your typing.

   b. Use a razor blade or a knife to scrape away as much carbon as possible without damaging the master. Remove any remaining carbon with a soft eraser. Type in the correction as in Step a.

   c. Apply correction tape to the back of the master sheet over the error to eliminate erasures completely. Then type the correction as in Step a.

1-10. Preparing a Master for Offset Duplication

1. Type on the emulsion side (the slick, shiny side).
2. Use a special offset ribbon. If your typewriter is equipped for carbonized ribbon, experiment with the various recommended paper and plastic ribbons until you find the one you like best.
3. Use a light touch; the object is to lay the image on the surface of the master without breaking through the emulsion.
4. To make corrections, use only a special offset eraser; use it with a light, blotting motion. *Do not break the surface of the master.*

1-11. Developing Good Typing Habits

1. Clean the typewriter regularly. (See page 1.)
2. Center the paper by properly adjusting the paper guide.
3. Use an even touch. On a manual typewriter, strike punctuation marks lightly.
4. Use a ribbon in good condition. The color of ink in the ribbon should harmonize with the letterhead copy.
5. Be accurate in typing, punctuating, capitalizing, spelling, hyphening, and dividing words. (See Units 8 to 12.)
6. Avoid strikeovers.
7. Keep the right-hand margin as even as possible.
8. Allow a sufficient margin at the bottom of the page. On a letter of two or more pages, allow at least a one-inch bottom margin.
9. Use uniform indentions:

   a. Five spaces are ordinarily used for paragraph indentions.
   b. Tabulated matter should be displayed attractively.
   c. Foreign or quoted material should vary in margin indentions from the basic form (usually being indented five more spaces).

10. Proofread every sheet before removing it from the typewriter.
11. Keep the typewriter centered and covered when it is not in use.
12. Do not attempt to make difficult repairs to your typewriter.

Letter Mechanics

While shortcuts in correspondence cannot be ignored, most businesses continue to use standard letter styles that employ the following components: heading, inside address, salutation, body, complimentary close, signature, and reference or identifying initials, and, sometimes, the attention line, the subject line, and (more often) the enclosure notation.

2-1. Heading

1. When a letterhead is used, the typed heading consists of the dateline only.

   a. Type the name of the month in full.

   b. Type the dateline to begin at the center of the page (for efficiency), to end flush with the right margin of the letter, or to balance with the letterhead.

   c. If block form is used, type the dateline flush with the left-hand margin. (See Letter 3-b on page 26.)

   d. Vertical placement on the dateline depends on the length of the letter if a floating dateline is used. (See the placement chart on page 34.)

Landscaping Company
144 Miami Drive   Rochester, N.Y. 14625   (716) 221-9045

March 7, 19--

2-a. Letterhead Showing the Date Beginning at Center

625 Burbank Drive, NW.   Atlanta, Georgia 30307   404-891-6563

March 7, 19--

**2-b. Letterhead Showing the Date Placed to End with
the Right Margin of the Letter**

2. If plain paper is used—as is many times the case in the writing of personal business letters—the information in the heading varies according to the purpose for which the letter is written. Generally, the heading should contain at least the post office address of the writer and the date. When the address is typed, two spaces should be left between the state name and the ZIP Code.

TWO-LINE HEADING

```
Burns, Kansas   66840
February 17, 19--
```

THREE-LINE HEADING

```
915 West Wisconsin Avenue
Adams, Wisconsin   53910
February 17, 19--
```

3. Certain types of correspondence, such as sales letters, advertising letters, and circular letters, occasionally justify the use of "special" datelines.

```
December                          June 23
Thirty-first                      1 9 - -
    19--
```

4. The inverted method of writing dates, which has been officially adopted by the military services, may be used in business correspondence. This style starts with the smallest unit (the day) and proceeds to the largest (the year) without any punctuation.

```
23 August 19--
```

5. In interoffice correspondence and memorandums (memos), numerical dates are permissible.

```
2/16/70 or 2-16-70
```

2-2. Inside Address

1. The business letter, unless it is a form letter or is semisocial in nature, always includes an inside address. The inside address in a business letter consists of at least the name of the individual or the name of the firm and the post office address.

2. The Post Office Department requests that ZIP Code numbers be included when sending mail. The ZIP Code number should be typed two spaces after the name of the state. No punctuation separates the ZIP Code number from the state name.

```
Milwaukee, Wisconsin   53203
Milwaukee, Wis.   53203
```

3. The state name may be spelled in full, abbreviated according to the standard abbreviation, or abbreviated according to the two-letter abbreviation recommended by the Post Office Department. If the latter abbreviation is used, the ZIP Code *must be used.* (See pages 131 and 132 for lists of state abbreviations.)

Mr. John Swift 700 Cliff Drive Tampa, Florida 33617	Mr. John Swift 700 Cliff Drive Tampa, Fla. 33617
Miss Susan Whitney 238 East 235 Street Euclid, Ohio 44123	Miss Susan Whitney 238 East 235 Street Euclid, OH 44123

4. Two or more lines are used for the inside address, depending upon the amount of information available. When only the city and state names follow the name of the addressee, two lines are used, with the addressee's name on the first line and with the city and state names and the ZIP Code on the second line.

Miss Judy White Withee, Wis. 54498	Miss Judy White Withee, WI 54498

5. Longer addresses may include such items as the name of the individual and his official position, the name of the firm, the name of the building, the street address, the city and state names, and the ZIP Code. This amount of information requires at least four lines.

Mr. Robert Lowe
Chicago School of Commerce
832 Market Avenue
Chicago, Illinois 60632

6. The inside address is blocked at the left margin.

7. Whether open or mixed punctuation is used, no end-of-line punctuation is used in the inside address except for an abbreviation.

8. An appropriate title should precede the name of the person. Standard titles for individuals are Mr., Mrs., Miss, and Ms. The corresponding plurals of the first three are Messrs., Mmes., and Misses. The title "Ms." may be used when writing to a woman whose marital status is unknown. This title may be applied to any woman, married or single; but it should be reserved for the woman whose title is not known.

Ms. Marianne MacIntosh

9. Some individuals should be addressed with special titles, such as Dr. (Doctor), Professor (Prof.), Honorable (Hon.), and Reverend (Rev.). While *Doctor* is usually abbreviated as a title, especially when the first name or the initials are used, the titles *Professor, Honorable,* and *Reverend* are written in full unless the name is too long.

```
    Dr. Homer Jones
or  William J. Loughrey, D.D.S.

    Professor Ward L. Brown
or  Prof. Lawrence R. Johnson

    The Honorable Lawrence Diersing
or  The Honorable Mr. Franecki

    The Reverend Mr. Frost
or  Reverend Thomas W. Groovis
or  Rev. William L. Hetherington
```

(For additional titles see Unit 5, page 37.)

10. Do not confuse the title with the official position. The title *precedes* the name in all instances. The official position, written in full, follows the name of the individual. However, some official titles because of common usage become personal titles. Examples are President Richard M. Nixon, Vice-President Spiro T. Agnew, Chief Justice Warren E. Burger.

11. The length of the individual's name or of the firm name determines whether the official position should be typed on the first or second line.

    a. When the official position is typed on the first line after the addressee's name, a comma precedes it.

    ```
    Mr. Clarence Heslar, Director
    Weldon Fabricating Co.
    Milwaukee, WI  53217
    ```

    b. If it is typed on the second line, the official position precedes the firm name, and it should be followed by a comma.

    ```
    Mr. Howard W. Hottenstein
    President, Riteway, Inc.
    Schenectady, NY  12332
    ```

    c. In some cases, the official position is of such length that a separate line will be required to type it.

    ```
    Dr. Paul A. Miller
    Superintendent of Schools
    930 East Ninth Street
    Cincinnati, OH  45202
    ```

12. Unusually long firm or corporate names may be typed on two lines, the second line being indented two or three spaces.

    ```
    Cincinnati Cooperative School
      of Technology
    3520 Central Parkway
    Cincinnati, OH  45223
    ```

13. Courtesy demands typing the name of the firm just as it appears in the letterhead. Whenever the ampersand (&) and the abbreviation for company (Co.) are used as part of the name, that style should be followed in the inside address.

14. Street names represented by the numerals one to ten, inclusive, are spelled out; from eleven on, use figures with or without the ordinal endings.

> 322 Sixth Street
> 439 North 13 Street
> 439 North 13th Street

15. If consecutive numbers are used to designate the address of the firm, they are separated by a hyphen.

> 1409-1427 Huntington Avenue

16. When the street name is a number and there is no intervening direction between it and the house number, a *space hyphen space* should separate the two items.

> 4309 - 18th Street

17. When the house or building number consists of the digit 1 (one), spell out "One"; use figures for the other single digits.

> One Hillcrest Avenue
> 8 Berkshire Lane

18. *North, East, South,* and *West* are usually not abbreviated when incorporated in street addresses. They *may* be abbreviated, however, to improve the balance of address lines.

> Mr. J. B. Kent
> 645 North Firestone Boulevard
> Akron, OH 44306
>
> Mr. J. B. Kent
> 645 N. Firestone Blvd.
> Akron, OH 44306

19. Compound sectional divisions of cities are abbreviated and follow street names.

> 384 Washington Avenue, S.E. (*or* SE *or* SE.)

2-3. Attention Line

1. The attention line, which is a part of the inside address, is typed two lines below the city and state names. It is used to assure delivery of the letter to a known individual within the organization.

2. The recommended placement of the attention line is even with the left margin, but it is sometimes centered.

3. No punctuation is needed after the word "Attention." It is usually not followed by "of." (See Letter 3-g on page 29.)

```
The Northern Construction Company
1516 Delaware Street
Cleveland, OH  44106

Attention Purchasing Agent

Gentlemen:
```

or

```
The Northern Construction Company
1516 Delaware Street
Cleveland, OH  44106

Attention Mr. Irvin C. Kuehn

Gentlemen:
```

2-4. Salutation

1. The salutation is typed two spaces below the last line of the inside address (or attention line if one is used) and flush with the left margin.

2. It may or may not be followed by a colon, but never by a comma in business writing.

3. Only the first word and all nouns in the salutation are capitalized.

```
Gentlemen:              Dear Mr. Fox:
My dear Sir             My dear Mrs. Watson
```

4. The choice of a salutation depends upon the first line of the inside address. The degree of formality existing between the correspondents determines the form of salutation to use.

    a. The salutation is a greeting to the recipient of the message. It is typed a double space below the address, if there is no attention line. The body of the letter begins a double space below the salutation. A salutation may be as informal as *Dear Bob* or as formal as *Sir.*

    b. The salutations given below are arranged from the least formal to the most formal.

FOR MEN

```
Dear Charles
My dear Charles:
Dear Mr. Hart:
My dear Mr. Hart:
Dear Sir:
My dear Sir:
Sir:
```

FOR A CORPORATION

```
Gentlemen:
```

FOR WOMEN

```
Dear Sharon:
My dear Sharon:
Dear Mrs. (Miss) Betts:
My dear Mrs. (Miss) Betts:
Dear Madam:
My dear Madam:
Madam:
```

FOR A FIRM OF WOMEN

```
Ladies:
Mesdames:
```

FOR A FIRM OF MEN

Gentlemen:

FOR A FIRM OF MEN AND WOMEN

Gentlemen:
Ladies and Gentlemen:
My dear Mrs. Dorr and Mr. Lane:

    c. *Dear Sirs* is outdated and is not acceptable as a substitute for *Gentlemen.*

    d. Personalized salutations, such as *Dear Mr. Sharp* and *My dear Miss Towne*, are replacing *Dear Sir* and *Dear Madam.* In social correspondence, *My dear Miss Towne* presupposes friendship. The reverse is true in business where the *My dear Miss Towne* or *My dear Mr. Sharp* is used when there is no acquaintanceship. The *Dear Miss Towne* or the *Dear Mr. Sharp* type of salutation suggests a business acquaintance that is real or exists because of previous correspondence.

> Mr. Arthur Havlovic
> Cincinnati Transit, Inc.
> 6 East Fourth Street
> Cincinnati, OH 45202
>
> Dear Mr. Havlovic:
>
>   *or*
>
> Cincinnati Transit, Inc.
> 6 East Fourth Street
> Cincinnati, OH 45202
>
> Attention Mr. Arthur Havlovic
>
> Gentlemen:

    e. Group mailings or promotional literature very frequently omit both the inside address and the salutation. Some firms have extended this idea by excluding the salutation and complimentary close on all correspondence. This is true of the AMS (Administrative Management Society, formerly National Office Management Association) type of correspondence and some streamlined styles adopted by individual firms. (See Letter 3-c on page 27.)

2-5. Subject Line

    1. When a subject line is used, it serves as a title to the content of the letter and should be typed two spaces below the salutation.

    2. The subject line may be typed flush with the left margin, centered, or begun at the paragraph point.

    3. Like the title of a story or a book, the subject line may include the topic only, although some writers prefer to prefix the word

Subject; others, more conservative perhaps, use *Re* or *In re* before the subject. If *Subject* is used, it should be followed by a colon.

(Flush with margin) Dear Mrs. Leonard:

    Re Zoller-Wynn Case, No. 94-6321-8

(Centered) Gentlemen:

       ACCOUNTING PROCEDURES

(Paragraph point) Dear Mr. Johnson:

    Subject: Military Status

    (See other illustrations, pages 27 and 31.)

2-6. Body

1. Begin typing the body of the letter two spaces below the salutation or two spaces below the subject line if one is used.
2. If the letter is typed in modified block style, paragraphs may or may not be indented. Paragraphs are not indented in the other standard letter styles.
3. When single spacing is used for the body of the letter, double-space between the paragraphs.
4. Paragraphing is one of the most effective means of securing reader attention. Since every paragraph represents a unit of related thought, it should be clear and brief so that the reader may grasp its meaning at a single glance.

 a. Avoid the two extremes—overparagraphing and underparagraphing.

 b. Long, lumbering paragraphs kill the reader's interest. Too many business letters are laid aside because of their cumbersome appearance.

 c. Variety in paragraph length increases appeal. If the message is divided into interesting, appealing paragraphs, it will still gain reader attention even though the actual wording of the letter is poor.

 d. Avoid, if possible, using the same number of lines in succeeding paragraphs.

 e. It is best to have in the letter a short opening and a short closing paragraph.

 f. Avoid writing just one line of a new paragraph at the bottom or at the top of a page.

g. Tabulate, if possible, two or more successive questions or statements that apply to the same unit of thought. (See Letter 3-c on
page 27.)

5. If any part of the dictated material lends itself to tabulation or to
display, allow space for tabulation or display by adjusting the
margin stops to allow for a writing line in the body of the letter
longer than is indicated in the letter placement chart on page 34.
Display adds to the attractiveness and effectiveness of the letter.
Single-space, indent, and center the quoted or tabulated matter.

6. Rather than allow the letter to have a crowded appearance, use a
second sheet. Plain stationery of the same quality and color as
the letterhead is used for second sheets. As a rule, it does not
carry any printed identification.

a. Plan the transcription of a two-page letter so that at least two
lines are carried over to the second page. It is better to retype
the letter than to use a second sheet for the complimentary close
and the signature alone.

b. For filing purposes, it is imperative that the second and succeeding pages carry an adequate identification or heading. This heading, typed about one inch from the top of the page, should
consist of the first line of the inside address, the date, and the
page number.

```
Mr. Richard L. Kiley--2          June 8, 19--
```

or

```
Mr. Richard L. Kiley
Page 2
June 8, 19--
```

or

```
Mr. Richard L. Kiley      2      June 8, 19--
```

c. Some organizations prefer to have the heading show the name
of the firm with the city and state, rather than the name of an
individual, even though the first line of the inside address carries
an individual's name.

```
Standard Oil Company--2          March 15, 19--
Newark, New Jersey   07101
```

d. Continue typing the letter, leaving two or three blank line spaces
between the heading and the resumed letter. (See illustrations on
pages 31 and 32.)

2-7. Complimentary Close

1. The complimentary close is the writer's way of saying "Good day,"
or "Good-bye." Its selection is determined by the salutation and
tone of the letter.

2. Where previous correspondence or some friendship exists, many correspondents prefer "Sincerely yours" or "Cordially yours."

3. Business sanctions the following combinations:

Salutation	VERY FORMAL	Complimentary close
Sir Reverend Sir Honorable Sir	Select one	Respectfully yours Yours respectfully Respectfully submitted

Salutation	FORMAL BUT WIDELY USED	Complimentary close
Dear Sir Dear Madam Ladies Gentlemen My dear Mr. Jones My dear Miss Smith	Select one	Very truly yours Yours very truly

Salutation	SEMIFORMAL	Complimentary close
Dear Mr. Jones Dear Miss Smith Dear Dr. Graham	Select one	Very sincerely yours Yours very sincerely Sincerely yours Yours sincerely Sincerely

Salutation	PERSONAL FRIENDSHIP	Complimentary close
My dear George Dear George	Select one	Cordially yours Yours cordially Cordially

Salutation	CLOSE CONFIDENTIAL RELATION	Complimentary close
My dear Jane Dear Jane	Select one	Faithfully yours Yours faithfully Faithfully

4. Only the first word of the complimentary close is capitalized.

5. No comma is used after the complimentary close if the colon has been omitted after the salutation.

6. Double-space between the body of the letter and the complimentary close.

2-8. Signature Lines

1. The content and sequence of the signature lines of a business letter are usually as follows:

a. Name of the company or firm (when used)
b. Penwritten signature of the dictator
c. Typewritten name of the dictator
d. Official position of the dictator

> **Note:** At one time the inclusion of the company name in the closing lines was considered to establish company responsibility, as opposed to individual responsibility, for the content of the message. Today, however, the company is considered responsible for the content of a message even though the company name does not appear in the signature lines.

2. When the company name is used in the closing lines (now a matter of mere preference), type it in solid caps a double space below the complimentary close. Type the name of the dictator and/or his official position four line spaces below the company name.

```
Sincerely yours          Very truly yours,

MEAD CORPORATION         THE KENDALL COMPANY, INC.
```

R. B. Littlejohn   *John C. Dunn*

```
R. B. Littlejohn         John C. Dunn, Manager
President
```

3. Some business concerns prefix *By* to the penwritten signature of any dictator who is not an official of the company.

```
Sincerely yours

THE BALTIMORE AND OHIO RAILWAY COMPANY
By    Martin L. Richter

Martin L. Richter, Agent
```

4. Most organizations prefer to omit the firm name from the closing lines in regular correspondence and to use the dictator's name with his official position. In such cases, type the name of the individual four line spaces below the complimentary close. The official position may be typed either beneath the typed name or on a line with it.

```
Sincerely yours          Very truly yours,
```

R. B. Littlejohn   *John C. Dunn*

```
R. B. Littlejohn         John C. Dunn, Manager
President
```

5. When the name of the dictator is not typed as a part of the signature, it should be written in the identification.

MAXWELL AND HOWE CO.

Howard A. Howe

District Superintendent

Howard A. Howe:EHF

6. When it is necessary for another person to sign the name of the dictator, that fact should be indicated in the signature or the identification.

    a. A common practice is to affix the initials of the signer.

Yours very truly

ACME INSURANCE COMPANY

John L. Newton DAK

District Manager

    b. Since many persons feel that the idea of having a secretary or other employee sign correspondence in the absence of the dictator tends to minimize the importance of the letter, firms are adopting a code or key plan by means of which the office may identify letters signed in this manner. The regular signature is used, but in the identification a key letter or figure appears along with the initials of the stenographer. In the illustration given below, the letter has been signed by a stenographer whose initials are *AC* and whose code number is *6*. If Mr. Goddard had signed the letter himself, the reference initials *AC* would have been used without the code number *6*.

Yours very truly,

AKRON RADIATOR COMPANY

Leslie I. Goddard

Sales Manager

Leslie I. Goddard: AC6

7. When the secretary has been requested to compose and sign a letter, she generally writes her name first followed by her official capacity. The illustration at the top of page 21 shows this type of signature.

Yours very truly,

Carolyn Hunt

Secretary to the President

8. If the employee holds no official title, she may sign her name and follow it with "For" and the name of the person for whom the letter was written.

Very truly yours,

Cecelia Johnson

For Mr. C. R. Wilson

9. An individual should adopt one style of signature and use that style consistently.

10. It is considered poor form to abbreviate the given name of an individual, such as *Geo.* for *George, Jas.* for *James,* or *Wm.* for *William.* If, however, an individual signs his correspondence in this manner, he should be addressed in this manner.

11. A man should never place *Mr.* or any other title before his signature.

Yours truly,   Cordially yours,

J. J. Kidd   *James N. Hilvert*

12. Signatures for women vary according to their status, but no woman should use initials *alone* when signing personal business communications. The business or professional woman who desires to retain her identity should establish a signature to be used in all business transactions. For example, although Sarah Hardding may be Mrs. Arthur Searle socially, she may retain her maiden name in the signature.

Sarah Hardding

13. The use of parentheses to enclose "Miss" or "Mrs." in a typewritten signature is optional. But there seems to be a growing tendency to omit the title *Miss* before names that are definitely feminine. In such instances as *Marion, Cecil, Billie, Shirley, Carol, Ora,* etc., where confusion may arise, it is better to indicate the title.

   a. When only a handwritten signature is used, enclose the title in parentheses.
   b. When used before the typed portion of the signature, the title need not be enclosed in parentheses.

Both of these styles are shown at the top of page 22.

Yours sincerely,   Yours very truly,

(Miss) Mary Robb   *Pamela Brelsford*

Miss Pamela Brelsford

14. The proper manner in which a married woman should sign her name is determined by the nature of the paper being signed. For *social* purposes, she should use her husband's name preceded by the title *Mrs.* in the typed signature. She should use her own first name in the handwritten signature.

   For business purposes, she should sign her own given name. For a middle name or initial, she may choose one of the following:

   Her own middle name
   The initial of her own middle name
   Her maiden surname
   The initial of her maiden surname

She will, of course, use her husband's surname.

   Suppose *Mary Alice Smith* marries *John Paul Jones.* For *social* purposes, she becomes *Mrs. John Paul Jones (Mrs. J. P. Jones, Mrs. J. Paul Jones, etc.).*

   For *business* purposes, she should use one of the following signatures:

```
Mrs. Mary Alice Jones
Mrs. Mary A. Jones
Mrs. Mary Smith Jones
Mrs. Mary S. Jones
```

15. A widow should prefix *Mrs.* in parentheses in the handwritten signature.

Yours very truly,

(Mrs.) Rose Calloway

16. The divorcee follows the form for the widow except in cases where the court has restored her maiden name. Then she uses the style of the unmarried woman.

Yours truly,   *or*   Yours sincerely,

(Mrs.) Jane Anders   *(Miss) Jane Royce*

17. When a woman signs a hotel register or endorses a government bond, check, or stock certificate, she should use the title *Miss* or *Mrs.* without parentheses. The government requires that a title be used before the payee's name, and of course the endorsement must correspond to that form.

18. Any portion of the signature enclosed in parentheses is explanatory
only. The purpose of such enclosure is to indicate to the recipient
the style that should be used when addressing further correspondence.

2-9. Identification

1. Identification or reference initials, the means of identifying the
dictator and the transcriber, are usually placed two spaces below
the last line of the typed signature and flush with the left margin.

2. If the letter does not carry an official title or the typewritten
name of the dictator, the name of the dictator and the initials of
the transcriber are typed five or six line spaces below the complimentary close and flush with the left margin.

3. No particular fixed style is required unless one is established by an
individual office.

a. The dictator's initials may precede the initials of the transcriber.

b. Modern usage favors the writing of the name of the dictator
followed by the initials of the transcriber.

c. In some offices numbers are assigned to the stenographers to
be used in lieu of reference initials.

```
LAL:AMK        RCB:GS           MFMcD/F
LEF            MH:jk            CRSmith-ak
DDL            ER               White 14
RMK-24         RMJones:DEF
```

4. In the complexities of business, occasions arise where two or more
persons may be specifically concerned with the construction of a
plan, a proposal, an estimate, etc. The office copy, at least, should
show this cooperative effort. This can be done by placing the intials
of all persons involved in addition to those of the transcriber in
the identification.

```
ABC-JKH/st     RED-LNO-STC: rexford     FAB:CRM:SRD
                                        wellner
```

2-10. Enclosures

1. When a letter carries a reference to an enclosure, the stenographer
should make a notation of the enclosure by writing *Enclosure* or
Enc. two spaces below the reference initials. If there are two
enclosures, he may write *Enclosures 2* or *Enc. 2.* (See Illustration 3-1 on page 31.)

2. Other notations, such as *Form 222, Check $178.50,* or *Catalog
mailed separately,* may follow the reference initials. (See Letter
3-i on page 30.)

3. Some firms list multiple enclosures as follows:

```
Enclosures:
    Report of June 30, 19--
    List of Salesmen
```

2-11. Carbon Copy Notations

1. When several carbon copies are made, reference to the recipient of each should be indicated as a special notation.
2. The names are generally arranged in the order of their importance. If all persons are of equal rank, arrange the names alphabetically.

```
cc Mrs. Kellogg              Copy to Mrs. Kellogg
cc Mr. Raiche      or        Copy to Mr. Raiche
```

2-12. Mailing .Notations

1. When a special postal service such as airmail, special delivery, or registered mail is to be used, add a mailing notation.
2. The mailing notation should be typed even with the left margin between the date line and the first line of the address.

2-13. Postscripts

1. Postscripts may be used to lend emphasis, because they are no longer considered afterthoughts. Types of information that can be used effectively in postscripts are the telephone number at the close of a letter of application, the restatement of an important thought taken from the body of the letter, or a statement that is entirely unrelated to the thought of the letter.
2. Postscripts should be brief. They may be used without the initials *P.S.* (See Letter 3-a on page 26.)

Illustrative Letters

The illustrative letters and their accompanying sheets, pages 26 to 32, contain examples of correct punctuation, style, and special features of letters.

3-1. Punctuation Styles

1. Open punctuation employs no special punctuation at the end of the dateline or at the end of any line of the inside address. It does not employ the colon after the salutation or the comma after the complimentary close.

2. Mixed punctuation follows the open style except for the use of the colon after the salutation and the comma after the complimentary close.

3-2. Special Features

FEATURE	LETTER NO.
1. A four-line address	3b, 3e, 3f
2. An attention line	3g
3. A subject line	3c, 3k
4. Unusual paragraphing	3d, 3e, 3f
5. Tabulation	3b, 3k, 3m
6. Special display lines	3d, 3g
7. Postscript	3a
8. Second sheet identification	3l, 3n
9. Carbon copy notation	3b
10. Enclosure notation	3g, 3i, 3l, 3n
11. Mailing notation	3b

American TRANSPORT COMPANY

Telephone 207-685-3384   500 North Saunders St.   Winthrop, Maine 04364

April 3, 19--

AIRMAIL

Mr. Eugene Krygowski
Krygowski Manufacturing Co.
208 Pitman Street
Elmhurst, IL 60126

Dear Mr. Krygowski:

Yes, we can supply you regularly with trailer-pulling service and guarantee three-day pickup service. We maintain three major motor pools; the midwest pool, which is located just outside Chicago, would serve you.

Our rates are based on a ton-mile formula: Multiply the number of tons (of cargo only) by the distance hauled to determine the number of ton miles; multiply that answer by our current rate (32 cents per ton-mile). The answer is your cost.

The runs you inquired about are listed in the following table:

Run Number	Average Tons	Miles	Ton Mile	Your Cost
1	10	152	1520	486.40
2	8	241	1928	616.96
3	4	20	80	150.00*
4	7	166	1162	371.84
5	6	342	2052	656.64
6	5	288	1440	460.80

*Minimum charge.

We are looking forward to serving you.

Yours very truly

J. T. Swinford
Sales Department

ck

Copy to Rate Department

SOUTHERN MARINE SUPPLY

700 Berkshire Lane
Chicago, Illinois 60624
(312) 221-0140

December 23, 19--

Mr. Herman Bryant
1446 Ziegler Avenue
Wheaton, IL 60187

Dear Mr. Bryant:

I am pleased to confirm May 22 as the delivery date for your new 32-foot "Starbrite" cruiser. The factory representatives assure me that the special options you ordered can be worked into their production schedule without any difficulty.

Our original quotation of $42,500 is now a firm price. It is payable at the time title is transferred.

You have selected a fine boat; I hope you will spend many enjoyable hours aboard.

Very truly yours,

J. R. Swartz, President

jh

As you know, a member of our staff will be available to assist you on a shakedown cruise at your convenience any time within 60 days of delivery.

STATE MUSIC COMPANY

432 Ladley Ave.   Evanston, Ill. 60204   (312) 871-6569

January 24, 19--

Dear Parent:

For those who understand and appreciate the finer things in life, the world of music is a delight that can last a lifetime.

Perhaps you yourself play an instrument or enjoy listening to music. Perhaps you have never cared much for music, but you recognize that your children should have an opportunity to enjoy music at an early age.

State Music provides a variety of instruments and services:

Instruments. STATE offers for sale or for rent the leading brands of stringed, brass, and percussion instruments.

Instruction. STATE has a staff of competent instructors who can provide expert guidance at convenient hours.

Music. STATE stocks a complete line of orchestrations, sheet music, and instruction books.

Supplies. STATE supplies all the incidental supplies necessary to keep your instrument in tip-top playing condition.

Records. STATE has a complete selection of record players and records.

Whatever your preference--classical, country and western, jazz, Dixieland, folk, band, orchestra, the newest or the oldest--stop by STATE and get your family into the swing of musical things!

Sincerely yours,

STATE MUSIC COMPANY

Stanley Lair

Stanley Lair, Manager

mt

3-d. Direct-Mail Style; Mixed Punctuation

Allied Office Equipment   116 Wieland Avenue   Brooklyn, New York 11202

September 12, 19--

Mrs. Judy Harper
Office Manager
Capozzolo, Inc.
1442 Northside Avenue
Orange, Calif. 92667

OFFICE SUPPLIES

The new era of business correspondence is here! Cleaner letter styles, more attractive letterheads and envelopes, new colored typewriter ribbons that produce a sharper impression, new type faces, postage meters, automatic letter openers--and many other innovations just as important--are available today.

The office manager is usually a busy person who puts off a trip to the stationer's store.

Perhaps you have been ordering the same old items by telephone and missing the chance to learn about all the newest things that are available. I would like to suggest one of two steps that will let you see what is new and that will take only a little of your valuable time.

1. Permit me to call on you, show you some of the new items, and leave a copy of our catalog, or

2. Simply call 242-3018 and have a catalog sent to you.

Either way, you will be opening the door to a new era of eye-pleasing correspondence and economical office appliances which make life in the office world more pleasant!

Lloyd Pitman

LLOYD PITMAN - SALES MANAGER

ch

3-c. AMS Simplified Style

Superior Jewelry

4309 Huntington Avenue   Willow Grove, Pennsylvania 19090   215-791-6364

August 22, 19--

Mrs. Barbara Sweeney
Penn Jewelry Co.
4193 Division Street
Mansfield, OH 44903

Dear Mrs. Sweeney

I am sure you will be interested in a preview of our new line for next year's market.

Wedding &
Engagement
Sets

The "Bridal Bouquet" set features new mountings for the stones that display even more vividly the unsurpassed brilliance you are accustomed to seeing in "Bridal Bouquet" sets. The wedding bands have been enhanced with a deep-etch, wider scroll design.

Watches

We have added two new brands, which promise to be best sellers this year. Announcements of new designs will be forthcoming in the next few weeks.

Men's
Jewelry

The expanded line of men's jewelry retains the solid appeal of real quality--with a special added dash to accentuate the new men's fashions.

Costume
Jewelry

The entire line of costume jewelry is new. All the sparkle and elegance of real gems and settings are available in inexpensive jewelry.

I shall be in Mansfield next week to show you all the fascinating new designs created for the coming year.

Sincerely yours

Charles E. Warman

Charles E. Warman
Sales Department

lf

3-f. Letter with Side Headings; Open Punctuation

ROSS STEEL CO. 449 Mill Road   Erie, Pennsylvania 16512   814-891-5996

March 13, 19--

Mr. I. E. Ziegler
Ziegler Construction Co.
311 Jones Street
Muskegon, MI 49443

Dear Mr. Ziegler:

Whenever a valued customer stops placing orders, we are naturally concerned. Have we failed in some way to serve you to your complete satisfaction? Have business conditions changed? Have you found a better or less expensive line of structural metals?

I would like very much to discuss with you some things I feel sure you will find interesting.

A new Michigan warehousing and distribution center will make available for same-day delivery virtually all of our structural forms.

A new automated order billing system will speed the handling of your orders and assure the accuracy of your invoices.

I shall be in Muskegon next Tuesday. May I talk with you then about several other new forms and services that we now have available?

Sincerely yours,

Donald E. Dadey

Donald E. Dadey
Sales Manager

cb

3-e. Inverted-Paragraph Style; Mixed Punctuation

PERSONAL DATA

Claire Kendall
275 East 235 Street
Euclid, Ohio 44123

Age: 24
Height: 5'7"
Weight: 125

Date: June 8, 19--
Nationality: Scotch
Church: Presbyterian

Education:

Commercial graduate, Southwest High School
Two years, University Extension Division
One year, Junior College (Evening School)

Experience:

Assistant to registrar during junior and senior years in high school

Two years as stenographer, Publication Department, American Medical Association

Two years as a case reporting and legal stenographer, Richards, Page, and Larkin, Attorneys-at-Law

References (by permission)::

Mr. Robert Richards
Suite 1432, Mariner Tower
Cleveland, Ohio 44118

Dr. David L. Howes
American Medical Association
1631 Abington Road
Cleveland, Ohio 44106

Mr. Lee R. Lane, Instructor
Junior College (Evening School)
Cleveland, Ohio 44118

Mr. Walter Kern
Southwest High School
Cleveland, Ohio 44123

3-h. Personal Data Sheet to Accompany Letter 3-g

---

275 East 235 Street
Euclid, Ohio 44123
June 8, 19--

Jones and Adams Company
2703 Lee Road
Cleveland, Ohio 44120

Attention Office Manager

Gentlemen:

Are you facing that vacation "double-up" inconvenience

--when the regular staff must assume additional responsibilities?
--when you work overtime yourself to keep routines on their daily schedule?
--when the potentialities of errors reach their all-season high?

Then you may be interested in knowing that there is available a person

--who has commercial skills such as stenography, typing, filing, use of Dictaphone, bookkeeping.
--who is adaptable.
--who enjoys the role of a substitute employee.
--who does not need to be told twice.
--who is alert and accurate.
--who has no designs on a permanent position.

Will you please read the attached personal data sheet for Claire Kendall to supplement these claims?

Please mark your calendar to call 731-9062 for an interview with an applicant for that summer vacancy.

Yours very truly,

Claire Kendall

Miss Claire Kendall

Enclosure

3-g. Letter of Application: Modified Block Style; Mixed Punctuation; Attention Line; Enclosure Notation

PERSONAL DATA SHEET

July 15, 19--

Electronics

Since taking my mechanical engineering degree at the University of California at Los Angeles in 19--, I have completed
a two-year Industrial Electronics Course in the University's
Evening School classes.

Instrumentation

On the job in the Development Department of the Morse Control
Company, San Francisco, I have had four years of design in
temperature, pressure, and humidity controls.

During this last year I have applied for three patents in
new designs of control elements.

Many of my original designs of pressure and temperature controls are in commercial production.

Personal

I am thirty years old, an American citizen, and single.
My present address is 35 Diaz Street, San Francisco, CA   94132.
My telephone number is 731-9886.

Education

San Mateo High School, San Mateo, California, 19--.
University of California, Los Angeles, California, 19--.
Further technical training includes the equivalent of a four-
year machinist's apprenticeship as well as three years in
tool design of instrument parts.

Employment

Morse Control Company since May, 19--.

References

My references will be submitted upon request.

3-j. Personal Data Sheet to Accompany Letter 3-i

---

35 Diaz Street
San Francisco, CA   94132
July 15, 19--

Tully Airplane Corporation
Research Department
742 Market Street
San Francisco, CA   94102

Gentlemen

    "Experience in the field of . . .:
     Electronics and Instrumentation"

Those qualifications prompt my asking you to consider
me for one of the openings at your Aeronautical Research
Center.

On the enclosed personal data sheet I have outlined my
qualifications that particularly refer to the type of
position you have available. In preparing the personal
data material, I have attempted to cover all the items
listed in your July 12 advertisement in the San Francisco
Beacon Journal.

I shall be glad to come in for an interview at any time
that is convenient for you. I shall appreciate the
opportunity of discussing my qualifications with you.

A telephone call to 731-9886 will reach me.

                    Very truly yours

                    Harry Leveridge

                    Harry Leveridge

cr

Enclosure: Personal Data Sheet

**3-i. Letter of Application: Modified Block Style; Open
Punctuation; Quotation; Enclosure Notation**

BRENTWOOD BB ROOFING CO.

4216 Miller Ave. Muskegon, Michigan 49444 (616) 741-4148

September 12, 19--

Henderson and Lowe, Architects
1645 Webster Road
Muncie, Indiana 47301

Gentlemen

Central High School Building

Since the subcontract for roofing on the Central High School project was awarded to us last May, our engineers have reviewed this week the original specifications. We find that several modifications of the specifications would facilitate the work and produce a better roofing job.

Specification 23 now reads in part as follows:

...and all other flashing of external fixtures and devices including but not limited to plumbing vents, electrical connections, and utility housings shall be sealed with bituminous roofing compound.

Our experience indicates that the new synthetic rubber sealants are far superior to the older bituminous compounds. The synthetic rubber sealant can be substituted at an increase in cost of only $200.

The original specifications call for three skylights:

    1 Sontage Model 24SLR
    2 Sontage Model 16SLR

Since the Sontage Manufacturing Company no longer markets either of these skylights, substitutions of similar units is indicated. For a well-made unit and prompt delivery, the following skylights are suggested:

    1 Easymount BLO24
    2 Easymount BLO16

The cost of these units would be the same as those originally specified.

Specification 27 calls for the use of Amalgum decorative tile on the mansard roof over the main entrance. Although this material

3-k. Two-Page Letter: Modified Block Style; Open Punctuation; Subject Line; Quoted Material; Tabulations

---

Henderson and Lowe, Architects
Page 2
September 12, 19--

is attractive and colorful, our experience with previous applications indicates that it tends to fade with exposure to the sun. Perhaps the decorative effect you desire could be achieved by using natural multicolored slate or ribbed copper. If the bright orange color is important, we would recommend the use of anodized aluminum roofing tiles. Cost would be:

    Natural slate $1,022 additional
    Ribbed copper   685 additional
    Anodized aluminum tile   468 additional

The enclosed descriptive material provides pictures and specifications of all materials suggested. Your early response will enable us to order materials at once and assure the completion of our part of the project on schedule.

Sincerely yours

William Bartell

William Bartell
President

cd

Enclosure

3-l. Second Page of Letter 3-k with Three-Line Second-Page Heading and Enclosure Notation

American Rental Inc.   119 Main Street   Durham, Conn. 06422   203-731-7325

November 2, 19--

Mr. Roy Anderson
347 Crest Circle
Chicago, Ill. 60624

Dear Mr. Anderson:

It was a pleasure to discuss with you the advantages of the AMERICAN RENTAL franchise plan. I was particularly pleased to receive your follow-up letter. The franchise plan has proven successful in many businesses; the AMERICAN RENTAL plan has already been employed successfully in many cities; there is every reason to believe that one or more AMERICAN RENTAL stores would thrive in Chicago.

Service to Contractors. The AMERICAN RENTAL plan makes available to large and small construction firms the equipment they need occasionally but cannot economically own and maintain themselves. Typical units stocked for the construction industry are as follows:

Concrete saws	Concrete breakers
Ditch diggers	Power rollers
Jack hammers	Concrete grinders
Power shovels	Sandblasters
Air compressors	Jumping jacks

Service to Homeowners. For the do-it-yourself homeowner, the AMERICAN RENTAL plan makes available tools that are needed only occasionally. Typical tools stocked for the do-it-yourself trade are as follows:

Rototillers	Circular saws
Mowers	Wheelbarrows
Edgers	Sewer cleaners
Seeders	Drills
Sprayers	Grinders
Lawn vacuums	Wallpaper steamers
Chain saws	Rug scrubbers
Log splitters	Floor polishers

AMERICAN RENTAL Franchise Service. The unique services of AMERICAN RENTAL make operation of a tool-rental business a smooth and profitable occupation. The intercity pool makes available to

3-m. Two-Page Letter: Modified Block Style; Mixed Punctuation: Subheadings: Tabulations

---

Mr. Roy Anderson   2   November 2, 19--

you and to your customer seldom-used tools from other franchise holders. Normally, any tool you need is available within 48 hours.

The promotion package offers advertising material developed by experts to promote your business in your city. The local advertising package, of course, ties in with the national advertising program.

The accounting package provides a ready-made system of inventory control, cash control, billing, and statement preparation. The preparation of financial statements and tax returns is part of the service.

The attractive, functional, prefabricated building package provides the best in physical facilities without duplication of planning effort and in the shortest possible time.

The AMERICAN RENTAL team of experts is available to each new franchise owner for as long as they are needed to establish every new store.

Please study the enclosed booklet carefully and let us hear from you when you are ready to enter the profitable world of AMERICAN RENTAL franchise owners!

Sincerely yours,

Joseph Ayer

Joseph Ayer, President

es

Enclosure

3-n. Second Page of Letter 3-m with One-Line Second-Page Heading and Enclosure Notation

Letter Placement

Letter placement should become an intuitive process. Until the eye has been trained to make accurate judgments, however, a placement table can be quite helpful. Placement of letters is based largely upon their length; but variation in letterheads, content, structure, and style must be taken into consideration when a setup is being planned. Every letter should be treated as an individual problem and should be handled in a manner to meet its specific purpose.

4-1. Letter Length

1. The intial step in letter placement is to recognize and classify the letter by length, whether you are transcribing from shorthand notes or from a dictating machine or are typing from rough draft or from copy written in longhand. Most placement tables classify letters as *short, average, long,* and *two-page*.
2. Tabulations, quoted material, subject and attention lines, and other unusual features increase the amount of space required by the letter. These features, therefore, must be considered in determining letter placement.

4-2. Differences in Pica and Elite Type

It is important that the typist recognize the difference between spaces per inch for pica and elite type.

1. On a typewriter with pica (large) type, there are 10 spaces to a horizontal inch.
2. On a typewriter with elite (small) type, there are 12 spaces to a horizontal inch.
3. Line length may be thought of and referred to as inches in margins or in spaces (or inches) per line.

Width of Margins	Spaces in Margins		Line Length	Spaces in Line	
	Pica	Elite		Pica	Elite
1″	10	12	6½″	65	78
1½″	15	18	5½″	55	66
2″	20	24	4½″	45	54

4-3. Centering the Paper

1. When standard-size stationery is used, the paper guide should be placed at "0" on the paper guide scale. The right and left margin

4-a. Short, Average, and Long Letters with Floating Dateline

stops should be equidistant from the center point (42 pica; 50 or 51 elite) to insure proper horizontal placement.

2. On some typewriters, "0" is the center point. If this is the case, the paper can be centered by setting the paper guide so that the readings on the paper-guide scale will be the same at both edges of the paper when the paper is inserted.

4-4. Floating Dateline Placement

1. This method of determining the placement of the typed letter on the page uses a *floating dateline*—a dateline that "floats" or varies in vertical position according to the letter length. This Reference Manual recommends the floating dateline placement because it is more widely used in business than the fixed date line.
2. The length of the letter determines (1) the line from the top edge of the paper on which the date is typed and (2) the width of the side margins (in inches).
3. The first line of the inside address is always typed on the fourth line below the date.

LETTER PLACEMENT TABLE (FLOATING DATELINE)

Letter Classification		5-Stroke Words in Letter Body	Side Margins	Margin Description	Dateline Position (From Top Edge of Paper)
Short		Up to 100	2"	Wide	Line 20
Average	1	101 – 150	1½"	Standard	18
	2	151 – 200	1½"	"	16
	3	201 – 250	1½"	"	14
	4	251 – 300	1½"	"	12
Long		301 – 350	1"	Narrow	12
Two-page		More than 350	1"	Narrow	12

BRENTWOOD ROOFING CO.
4716 Miller Ave. Muskegon Michigan 49444 (616) 741-6148
March 15, 19--

National Insurance Company
1545-49 American Building
229 East Baltimore Street
Baltimore, MD 21202

Attention Office Manager

Gentlemen

Sincerely yours

Richard E. Adams
President

jwr

PD PERRY & DERRICK, INC.
111 Lincoln Park / Newark, New Jersey 07102
March 15, 19--

Illinois Casualty Company
37 South Wabash Avenue
Chicago, IL 60603

Gentlemen

Improving Business Communications

Sincerely yours

Alfred B. Williams
Vice-President

rm
Enclosure
cc Mrs. Lee Seipelt

GIBBS ASSOCIATES
330 N. Michigan Avenue
Chicago, Illinois 60601
March 15, 19--

Mr. Kevin McMahon, Director
American Business Institute
One Fifth Avenue
New York, NY 10003

Dear Mr. McMahon:

Very truly yours,
GIBBS ASSOCIATES

John E. Homan, Manager

lrb
cc Mr. Paul McCarthy

4-b. Short, Average, and Long Letters with Fixed Dateline

4. If adjustment in letter placement is necessary because of special features (attention and subject lines, long quotations, listed enumerations), you can adjust the placement of the letter by:

a. Raising the dateline (and the body of the letter with it).

b. Decreasing the space between the closing lines and between the special guide lines at the lower left of the letter.

5. Letter placement can sometimes be improved for letters at the low end of a length classification by increasing the space between the closing lines and the special guide lines.

4-5. Fixed Dateline Placement

1. This method of determining the placement of the typed letter on the letterhead uses a *fixed dateline*—a dateline that is always typed on the second line below the last line of the printed letterhead.

LETTER PLACEMENT TABLE (FIXED DATELINE)

Letter Classification	5-Stroke Words in Letter Body	Variable Margins			Standard 60-Space Line
		Length of Line		Blank Lines Between Dateline and Address **	Blank Lines (Average) Between Dateline and Address **
		Pica Spaces	Elite Spaces		
Short	Fewer than 100	50*	50*	7–11	8
Average	101–200	60*	60*	3–7	5
Long	201–300	60	70	3–5	3
Two-page	More than 300	60	70	3–5	3

* When it is necessary to change the length of line from a 50-space line to a 60-space line, just move each margin stop out 5 spaces; time can be saved in a similar way when it is necessary to shorten the length of the line.
** Letters at the extremes of the classifications, in terms of the number of words in the body of the letter, may at times require some modification of the suggested spacing between the dateline and the address.

2. The length of the letter determines (1) the number of blank lines to be left between the date line and the inside address and (2) the length of the lines; that is, the number of spaces in the lines of the letter.

3. If adjustment in letter placement is necessary because of special features, you can adjust the placement of the letter by:

   a. Increasing or decreasing the number of line spaces between the date and the first line of the inside address.

   b. Increasing or decreasing the line spaces used in the closing lines and between the special guide lines at the lower left of the letter.

Titles and Salutations

Titles are words of courtesy. They are used before the names of individuals in inside and envelope addresses. These titles are selected according to the status of individuals. There are professional and scholastic titles, religious titles, and titles for government officials and military personnel. All titles except *Esq.* precede the name. The choice of the title generally influences the salutation, and the salutation in turn controls the choice of the complimentary close.

5-1. Titles of Individuals

NAME	EXPLANATION	SALUTATION
Mr. Ballard Morris	A man	Dear Sir: * My dear Sir: Dear Mr. Morris: * My dear Mr. Morris:
Master Martin Wallace	A boy younger than a teen-ager	Dear Master Wallace: Dear Martin:
Mrs. William Stith *or* *Mrs.* Mary Stith	A married woman or a widow	Dear Madam: * My dear Madam: Dear Mrs. Stith: * My dear Mrs. Stith:
Miss Bernice Price	An unmarried woman	Dear Madam: * My dear Madam: Dear Miss Price: * My dear Miss Price:
Ms. Bernice Price	Marital status unknown	Dear Ms. Price:
Messrs. Able and Baker	Two or more men	Gentlemen:
Rand & Smith Co.	Firm composed of men and women	Gentlemen: Ladies and Gentlemen Dear Mr. Rand and Mrs. Smith:
Mmes. Lee & Gans *or* Blake Incorporated	Two or more married women or a firm of women	Ladies: Mesdames:
The *Misses* Bell *or* *Misses* Ann and Ada Bell *or* The *Misses* Ann and Ada Bell	Two or more unmarried women	Ladies:
Mr. and *Mrs.* John Farr	A man and his wife	Dear Mr. and Mrs. Farr:

* Formal salutation.

NAME	EXPLANATION	SALUTATION
Dr. and *Mrs.* F. J. Schultz	A doctor and his wife	Dear Dr. and Mrs. Schultz:
Joseph Addison, *Esq.*	Formerly an English title denoting a person of high position. It is now used as the equivalent of *Mr.,* particularly when addressing an attorney. It is placed after the name and is always abbreviated.	Dear Sir: * My dear Sir: Dear Mr. Addison: * My dear Mr. Addison:

5-2. Professional or Scholastic Titles

NAME	EXPLANATION	SALUTATION
Dr. David Horne	Used with the name of any person having a degree containing the letter *D*; as, *M.D., LL.D., D.D., Ph.D., D.D.S., Ed.D.,* etc.	Dear Sir: * My dear Sir: Dear Dr. Horne: (or Doctor) * My dear Dr. Horne:
Professor Edward Adams *or* *Prof.* Edward Adams	One holding a professorship in a college or a university. When the given name is used in the inside address, *Prof.* is acceptable.	Dear Sir: * My dear Sir: Dear Professor Adams: * My dear Professor Adams:

1. Degree designations should always follow the name. They are always abbreviated and normally lend authority and dignity to the correspondence. (See Unit 14, page 129.)
2. When a professional degree is used, no title should appear before the name.

Robert A. Curtis, M.D.   *or*   Dr. Robert A. Curtis

5-3. Religious Titles

1. Roman Catholic Faith

THE POPE	SALUTATION
His Holiness Pope Paul VI Vatican City Rome, Italy	Your Holiness: Most Holy Father:

A CARDINAL	SALUTATION
His Eminence, John Cardinal Dearden Archbishop of Detroit 1880 Wellesley Drive Detroit, Michigan 48203	Your Eminence: Dear Cardinal Dearden:

---

* Formal salutation.

AN ARCHBISHOP

The Most Reverend Paul F. Leibold   Your Excellency:
Archbishop of Cincinnati
The Chancery
29 East Eighth Street
Cincinnati, Ohio   45202

A BISHOP   SALUTATION

The Most Reverend John Muldoon   Your Excellency:
Bishop of Oklahoma   Dear Bishop Muldoon:
Oklahoma City, Oklahoma   73102

MEMBERS OF THE CLERGY

Monsignor

The Right Reverend Joseph Ryan   Right Reverend and dear
St. Brendan's Church   Monsignor:
Chicago, Illinois   60606   Dear Monsignor Ryan:

Priest

The Reverend William R. Rand   Reverend and dear Sir:
St. Joseph's Rectory   Dear Father Rand:
164 Lansing Place
Mobile, Alabama   36627

Brother of a Catholic order

Brother Brendon, O.F.M.   Dear Brother:
St. Francis Seminary   Dear Brother Brendon:
Quincy, Illinois   62301

RELIGIOUS ORDERS OF WOMEN

Reverend Mother Mary Louise, O.C.A.   Reverend Mother:
Sacred Heart Convent   Dear Reverend Mother:
New Orleans, Louisiana   70108

Sister Mary Margaret   Dear Sister:
St. Catherine's School   Dear Sister Mary Margaret:
Rochester, Minnesota   55901

2. Protestant Faith

A BISHOP (EPISCOPALIAN)   SALUTATION

The Right Reverend A. B. Clark   Right Reverend and dear
Bishop of New York   Sir:
The Bishop's House   My dear Bishop Clark:
New York, New York   10010   Dear Bishop Clark:

A DEAN (EPISCOPALIAN)

Dean Malcolm D. Maynard   Sir:
All Saints' Cathedral   Very Reverend Sir:
Milwaukee, Wisconsin   53202

A MINISTER   SALUTATION

The Reverend Andrew G. Finnie   Reverend Sir:
Immanuel Presbyterian Church   My dear Sir:
Milwaukee, Wisconsin   53202   Dear Sir:
                                        My dear Mr. Finnie:
                                        Dear Mr. Finnie:

RELIGIOUS ORDERS OF WOMEN

Episcopalian

Sister Ethelreda   Dear Sister Ethelreda:
All Saints' Cathedral Guild Hall
818 East Juneau Avenue
Milwaukee, Wisconsin 53202

Lutheran

Sister Emma   Dear Sister Emma:
Milwaukee Hospital
Milwaukee, Wisconsin 53202

3. Jewish Faith

A RABBI

Rabbi Dudley Weinberg   Sir:
Congregation Emanu-El B'ne Jeshurun   My dear Dr. Weinberg:
Milwaukee, Wisconsin 53211   My dear Rabbi:
                                           My dear Rabbi Weinberg:

5-4. Titles of Government Officials

PRESIDENT OF THE UNITED STATES   SALUTATION

The President   Sir:
The White House   Mr. President:
Washington, D.C. 20500   Dear Mr. President:
                                           My dear President Nixon:

The Honorable Richard M. Nixon
President of the United States
The White House
Washington, D.C. 20500

VICE-PRESIDENT OF THE UNITED STATES   SALUTATION

The Vice-President   Sir:
United States Senate   My dear Sir:
Washington, D.C. 20510   Dear Sir:
                                           Mr. Vice-President:
The Honorable Spiro T. Agnew   My dear Mr. Vice-President:
The Vice-President of the United
   States
Washington, D.C. 20510

CHIEF JUSTICE OF THE UNITED STATES   SALUTATION

The Chief Justice   Sir:
The Supreme Court   Mr. Chief Justice:
Washington, D.C. 20543   Dear Mr. Chief Justice:

The Honorable Warren Burger
Chief Justice of the Supreme Court
   of the United States
Washington, D.C. 20543

ASSOCIATE JUSTICE OF THE SUPREME COURT

Mr. Justice Potter Stewart
The Supreme Court of the United
  States
Washington, D.C.   20543

The Honorable Potter Stewart
Associate Justice of the Supreme Court
Washington, D.C.   20543

SALUTATION

Sir:
Mr. Justice:
My dear Mr. Justice:
My dear Justice Stewart:
Dear Justice Stewart:

SPEAKER OF THE HOUSE

The Speaker of the
  House of Representatives
Washington, D.C.   20515

The Honorable John W. McCormack
Speaker of the House of
  Representatives
Washington, D.C.   20515

SALUTATION

Sir:
My dear Sir:
Dear Sir:
Mr. Speaker:
My dear Mr. Speaker:
Dear Mr. Speaker:
My dear Mr. McCormack:
Dear Mr. McCormack:

MEMBER OF THE CABINET

The Secretary of State
Washington, D.C.   20502

The Honorable William P. Rogers
Secretary of State
Washington, D.C.   20502

SALUTATION

Sir:
My dear Sir:
Dear Sir:
My dear Mr. Secretary:
Dear Mr. Secretary:

SENATOR (MALE)

The Honorable Clifford P. Hansen
The United States Senate
Washington, D.C.   20510

Senator Clifford P. Hansen
The United States Senate
Washington, D.C.   20510

SALUTATION

Sir:
My dear Sir:
Dear Sir:
My dear Mr. Senator:
My dear Senator:
Dear Senator:
My dear Senator Hansen:
Dear Senator Hansen:

SENATOR (FEMALE)

The Honorable Margaret Chase Smith
The United States Senate
Washington, D.C.   20510

Senator Margaret Chase Smith
The United States Senate
Washington, D.C.   20510

SALUTATION

Madam:
My dear Senator Smith:
Dear Madam:
My dear Madam Senator:
Dear Mrs. Smith:

REPRESENTATIVE (MALE)

The Honorable Robert Taft
The House of Representatives
Washington, D.C.   20515

Representative Robert Taft
The House of Representatives
Washington, D.C.   20515

SALUTATION

Sir:
My dear Sir:
Dear Sir:
My dear Representative Taft:
My dear Congressman:
Dear Mr. Taft:

REPRESENTATIVE (FEMALE)	SALUTATION
The Honorable Patsy T. Mink The House of Representatives Washington, D.C. 20515	Madam: My dear Mrs. Mink: Dear Madam:
Representative Patsy T. Mink The House of Representatives Washington, D.C. 20515	Dear Representative Mink: Dear Mrs. Mink:

A STATE REPRESENTATIVE	SALUTATION
The Honorable Michael Maloney Senate Office Building Columbus, Ohio 43215	Sir: Dear Sir: Dear Mr. Maloney: My dear Mr. Maloney:

A MAYOR	SALUTATION
The Honorable Richard J. Daley Mayor of the City of Chicago Chicago, Illinois 60601	Sir: Dear Sir: My dear Mayor Daley: Honorable Sir:

5-5. Titles of Military Personnel

1. Consult the *Official Registers* of the armed services to obtain current listings of divisions and classifications.

2. All officers, whether commissioned or noncommissioned, are addressed by their titles. Other members of the services should have the name prefixed by the rank.

3. The address of the commissioned officer should include:

> Line 1 Title and Name of Officer
> Line 2 Station
> Line 3 Service Address (City, State, or County)

ADDRESS	SALUTATION
Captain David H. Kemp Ft. Knox Ft. Knox, Ky. 40121	Sir: My dear Captain Kemp:

4. For the address of the noncommissioned officer and other personnel, follow this style:

> Line 1 Title and Name
> Line 2 Serial and Number
> Line 3 Station
> Line 4 Service Address (City, State, or Country)

ADDRESS	SALUTATION
Pfc. Robert A. Jaeger U.S. 68-129-680, Hq. & Hq. Co. Bossier Base Shreveport, Louisiana 71110	Dear Pfc. Jaeger

Tabulation

Tabulation is the arrangement of information in a concise, systematic, and artistic manner. Its purpose is to present facts and figures conveniently and clearly. Compactness is basic to good tabulation. Difficult tabulations must be planned before they are typed in order to save time, materials, and energy. In fact, a rough draft may be a necessary first step. All tabulations require a knowledge of centering, both vertical and horizontal.

In this unit, three methods of arranging tabulations, along with a listing of tabulation techniques, are presented. The mathematical plan is especially useful in involved, cumbersome problems; while the backspace-from-center plan is an extension of the method used for centering headings.

6-1. The Mathematical Plan

1. To determine the vertical placement—

a. Determine the total number of horizontal lines available for typing. (A standard sheet, 8½ x 11 inches, has 66 lines.)

b. Decide upon the number of lines needed for the tabulation, blank lines as well as typed lines.

c. Subtract the number of necessary lines (Step *b*) from the number of lines available for typing (Step *a*).

d. Divide the result obtained in Step *c* by 2 to find the number of line spaces in equal top and bottom margins.

e. If the tabulation is to be typed in reading position, subtract 2 lines from the result obtained in Step *d* to determine the top margin.

f. Begin the typing on the line below the last line in the top margin. For example, if the top margin is to have 20 line spaces, begin typing on Line 21.

2. To determine the horizontal placement—

a. Determine the total number of horizontal spaces available for typing. (A standard sheet, 8½ x 11 inches, has 85 pica or 102 elite spaces.)

b. Decide upon the number of columns needed.

c. Ascertain the number of spaces needed to type the longest item in *each* column. (The heading may be the longest line in a column.) Add these numbers.

d. Subtract the total number of spaces needed to type the longest items in all the columns (Step *c*) from the total number of spaces available for typing (Step *a*).

e. Divide the result obtained in Step *d* by the number of columns needed (Step *b*) plus one. This figure gives you the position of the left-hand margin stop and also the number of spaces to be left between columns.

f. From the left-hand margin, space forward once for every letter in the longest item of the first column plus the number of spaces to be left between columns. Set a tab stop here for the second column.

g. Repeat Step *f* until tab stops have been set for all columns.

h. Start at left-hand margin and type the tabulation horizontally line by line.

6-2. The Backspace-from-Center Plan

1. The vertical placement of the tabulated material should be determined as outlined under the mathematical plan.
2. To determine the horizontal placement—

   a. Decide upon the number of columns needed.
   b. Decide upon the number of spaces to be left between columns. Use an even number of spaces, such as 4, 6, or 8.
   c. Start at the center point and backspace once for every two letters and spaces in the longest item of each column plus once for every two spaces between columns.
   d. Set the left-hand margin stop at this point—the beginning of the first column.
   e. Space forward the number of spaces required to type the longest item of the first column plus the number of spaces between columns. Set a tab stop here for the second column.
   f. Repeat Step *e* until tab stops have been set for all columns.
   g. Start at the left-hand margin and type the tabulation horizontally line by line.

6-3. Tabulation Placement Chart

By following the steps below, horizontal placement of tabulations may be planned without calculations.

1. Choose the proper table (pica or elite). (See page 45.)
2. Select the number of columns that will be typed.
3. Select the number of spaces required to type the longest items in all the columns (you may not find the exact number; choose the closest one).
4. On the chart on page 45, match the total number of spaces in the longest items of all the columns with the number of columns. The block where these two intersect establishes the left margin.
5. Set the left margin stop; thumb-space the number of spaces in the first column plus ten (six if you are using a pica typewriter); set a tab stop for the second column; thumb-space the number of spaces in the second column plus ten (six if you are using a pica typewriter); set a tab stop, etc.

ELITE TYPE—10 SPACES BETWEEN COLUMNS

Total Spaces	5	10	15	20	25	30	35	40	45	50	55	60	65	70	75	80
Columns																
2	43	41	38	36	33	31	28	26	23	21	18	16	13	11	9	6
3	38	36	33	31	28	26	23	21	18	16	13	11	9	6	—	—
4	33	31	28	26	23	21	18	16	13	11	9	6	—	—	—	—
5	28	26	23	21	18	16	13	11	9	6	—	—	—	—	—	—
6	—	21	18	16	13	11	9	6	—	—	—	—	—	—	—	—
7	—	16	13	11	9	6	—	—	—	—	—	—	—	—	—	—
8	—	11	9	6	—	—	—	—	—	—	—	—	—	—	—	—

PICA TYPE—6 SPACES BETWEEN COLUMNS

Total Spaces	5	10	15	20	25	30	35	40	45	50	55	60	65	70	75	80
Columns																
2	37	34	32	29	27	24	22	19	17	14	12	9	7			
3	34	32	29	27	24	22	19	17	14	12	9	7	—			
4	31	28	26	23	21	18	16	13	11	9	6	—	—			
5	28	25	23	21	18	16	13	10	8	—	—	—	—			
6	25	22	20	17	15	12	10	7	—	—	—	—	—			
7	22	19	17	14	12	9	7	—	—	—	—	—	—			
8	19	16	14	11	9	6	—	—	—	—	—	—	—			

6-4. The Judgment or "Guesswork" Plan

1. This plan is adaptable to simple tabulations.

2. The typist uses his own judgment as to how many lines to leave for the top margin, width of side margins, and spacing between columns.

6-5. Tabulation Techniques

1. Choose a short, clear, main heading or title.

2. Center and type the main heading entirely in caps.

3. Center each columnar heading in relation to the width of the column below it. Capitalize the first and all important words in a columnar heading.

4. Omit punctuation after titles and/or columnar headings.

5. Type tabulations line by line, not column by column.

6. Place a dollar sign before the first figure and the total figure in every column when necessary for clarity. The dollar sign should be placed so that it would be in the correct position for the longest item in the column if it were typed before that longest item.

7. Use the decimal point only when there are figures to the right of it in some lines.

$346.00	$ 635		$ 635.
273.36	26	*not*	26.
429.37	1,169		1,169.

8. Insert a cipher to the left of the decimal point when the first number in the column or under a cross ruling is a decimal fraction.

1.48		1.48
0.92	*not*	.92
2.50		2.50

9. Repeat the headings if a tabulation extends to the second page.

SALES QUOTAS BY DISTRICTS

Central City	Equipment	Supplies and Miscellaneous
Cincinnati, Ohio	$105,000	$12,650
Chicago, Illinois	362,416	27,840
Dallas, Texas	111,680	13,482
New York, New York	381,751	41,693
Seattle, Washington	196,470	21,642

6-a. A Properly Planned Tabulation

Note that the spaces between columns (not headings) are equalized.

Grammar—The Mainspring of Communications

One is judged by the skill with which he communicates ideas. Anyone who works with business correspondence is expected, as a minimum, to use words correctly. Few business firms can afford to tolerate errors in spelling or grammar. Beyond these minimum requirements, the *successful* business correspondent must gain a knowledge of *rhetoric*—the effective, successful use of words.

The *minimal* secretary can transcribe a letter if it is dictated word for word, comma for comma. The *skilled* secretary uses her own judgment to produce a finished letter when a skeletal outline is dictated. The *real expert* needs to be told only the basic idea. She can compose a complete, tactful, accurate letter from such instructions as, "Tell him no" or "Tell him no on the first, yes on the second."

The following guides point out some common pitfalls. This section may be used as an aid in overcoming those faulty language patterns which most frequently hinder effective expression.

7-1. Agreement of the Verb with the Subject

1. The subject, as a rule, is a noun or a pronoun. Nouns may be singular or plural in number, compound or collective in nature. The verb must agree with the subject in both person and number.

2. A singular noun requires a singular verb; a plural noun requires a plural verb.

     One spacecraft *is* (not *are*) orbiting the moon.
     Three astronauts *are* (not *is*) aboard.

3. A compound subject requires a plural verb.

     Boys and girls *are* (not *is*) in line.
     Bill and Mary *don't* (not *doesn't*) go together.

4. When two words of a compound subject refer to the same person or thing, the verb is singular.

     A friend and counselor *is* (not *are*) a boon to an invalid.
     A friend and a counsel *are* (not *is*) needed.

5. With *either-or* and *neither-nor,* the singular is used when both nouns are singular; otherwise the verb agrees with the subject

nearer it. When a singular and a plural form appear in the subject, place the plural nearer the verb and use a plural verb.

> Either Tom or Jill *is* (not *are*) going.
> Neither he nor they *were* (not *was*) included.

6. When pronouns require different verb forms, the correct one is used with each subject.

> Either he *is* going or I *am*.

7. Collective nouns take singular verbs when the groups act as units and plural verbs when the members of the groups act individually.

> The committee *recommends* (not *recommend*) a complete re-organization.
> The committee *were* (not *was*) asked to order their lunches.

8. Nouns that are plural in form but singular in meaning take singular verbs.

> Economics *is* (not *are*) an interesting subject.
> News *is* (not *are*) scarce.

9. Nouns plural in form and collective or plural in meaning take plural verbs.

> Things *were* (not *was*) not as they seemed.
> The goods *are* (not *is*) being shipped today.

10. Quantities, sums of money, and periods of time used as a unit require singular verbs.

> Five inches *is* (not *are*) the length.
> Ten days *is* (not *are*) too long to wait.

11. A fraction takes a singular verb unless the phrase following has an object that is plural in number.

> Two thirds of the fund *has* (not *have*) been used.
> Three fourths of the ships *are* (not *is*) at sea.

12. The word *number* preceded by *the* takes a singular verb; when preceded by *a*, the word *number* always takes a plural verb.

> The number of lost books *is* (not *are*) surprisingly small.
> A number of lost books *have* (not *has*) been found.

13. Words such as *rest, abundance, plenty,* and *variety* are controlled by the object of the phrase that modifies the word.

> The rest of the tourists *were* (not *was*) housed in motels.
> The rest of the report *is* (not *are*) available to the public.

14. Subjects containing *each, every, anybody, nobody, anything, no one, someone, everybody,* and *everyone* require single verbs.

> Every candidate *is* (not *are*) allowed TV time.

15. When *all, any, more, most, some, that, what, who, which,* or *none*
is the subject of a sentence, a singular or plural verb may be used,
depending upon the reference.

> All *has* been stolen. (a quantity in singular sense)
> All the letters *were* typed. (a quantity in plural sense)
> None of the men *were* asked to sign the petition. (plural sense)
> Who *is* going to accompany you? (what person)

16. *Both, few, several,* and *many* require plural verbs.

> Both students *were* (not *was*) given recognition.
> Several *have* (not *has*) not been questioned.

17. In a sentence beginning with *there is* or *there are,* the subject follows and controls the verb.

> There *is* (not *are*) a post at the corner.
> There *are* (not *is*) many posts on the east side.

18. Subjects, not intervening words or phrases, control the number of
the verb.

> Walking to work on Mondays *is* (not *are*) a long-standing habit.
> Taxes, in addition to interest, *are* (not *is*) considered in arrang-
> ing installment payments.

7-2. Use of Pronouns

1. Pronouns present the problems of person, number, gender, and
case. Pronouns may be used in the first, second, or third person;
singular or plural in number; masculine, feminine, or neuter in
gender; nominative, possessive, or objective in case.

PERSONAL PRONOUNS

Case	*Singular*	*Plural*
Nominative	I, you, he, she, it	we, you, they
Possessive	my, mine, your, yours, his, her, hers, its	our, ours, your, yours, their, theirs
Objective	me, you, him, her, it	us, you, them

RELATIVE PRONOUNS

Nominative	who	which	that	what
Possessive	whose	whose	whose	. . .
Objective	whom	which	that	. . .

2. The nominative case is used where the pronoun is a subject or a
predicate noun.

> *It* is *she.*
> *It* should not have been *they.*
> He should employ *whoever* is best qualified. (subject of verb *is*)
> *Who* is going with you?

3. The possessive case is used where the pronoun shows ownership, origin, or kind.

> *His* memory fades frequently.
> Can we count on *your* taking the job?
> *Whose* books are these?

4. The objective case is used where the pronoun is the object of a verb or preposition or where the pronoun is the subject of an infinitive.

> The car accident maimed *him* permanently. (object of verb *maimed*)
> The argument was between *you* and *her*. (object of preposition *between*)
> The firm should employ *whomever* it chooses. (object of verb *chooses*)
> Ask her to *whom* she is writing. (object of preposition *to*)
> *Whom* would you expect to see? (object of phrase *to see*)
> The regulars expected *him* to be present at the meeting. (subject of infinitive *to be*)

5. Personal pronouns must agree in number with their antecedents.

> The *audience* votes on the program *it* approves. (singular)
> The *audiences* cast *their* votes after the show. (as individuals)
> The *lawyer* and his *clients* enjoyed *their* outing. (plural)

6. When the antecedent involves persons of both sexes, the masculine personal pronoun is used.

> *Everyone* must look after *his* own supplies.

7. *Who* refers to persons; *which,* to things; *that,* to persons or things. Specifically, *that* should be used when referring to animals, with collective nouns, and when both persons and things are concerned.

> This is Tom, *who* is a detective.
> This is a car *which* will give good service.
> The cat *that* was frightened climbed the tree.
> Was it the captain or the storm *that* determined the course?

8. Indefinite pronouns (*one, anyone, someone, somebody,* etc.) are singular; pronouns that refer to them must be singular.

> As *one* sows, so shall *he* reap.

> **Note:** One should not use *you* as an indefinite pronoun. Substitute *one, anyone,* etc.

7-3. Misuse of Common Words and Verb Phrases

1. Many errors stem from the failure to recognize the shades of meaning of words that are similar in sound but different in spelling. See the list of such words on pages 100-104 of Unit 10.
2. Irregular verbs are the source of many errors. They present the problem of choosing the right verb form and the correct auxiliary

or helping verb if one is needed. The principal parts of a few of the common irregular verbs follow:

PRESENT	PAST	PAST PARTICIPLE
come	came	come
do	did	done
go	went	gone
lie (*to rest*)	lay	lain
lay (*to place*)	laid	laid
see	saw	seen

a. Auxiliary or helping verbs are always used with the past participle. These verbs are forms of *to be* (*is, are, was, were, been*); forms of *have* (*has, had*); and *could, should,* and *would.*

> Old clothes *were worn* (not *were wore*) at the party.
> They *have gone* (not *have went*) to see the town.
> The rains *have done* (not *have did*) the damage.
> She *should have worn* (not *should have wore*) her work clothes.

b. *Lie, lay,* and *lain* represent resting or reposing and do not require an object; *lay, laid,* and *laid* represent placing or the "putting down" of something and require an object.

> Please *lie* (not *lay*) down to rest.
> He *lay* (not *laid*) under the tree for some time.
> The student has *laid* (not *lain*) his book on the desk.

c. *Of* is not to be used for *have* with *may, might, must, could, should, would,* or *ought to.*

> He *could have* (not *could of*) run the race.
> They *should have* (not *should of*) gone home by now.

3. Among the common word errors are the interchange of adjectives and adverbs and the misunderstanding of their application. Comparisons often cause word errors.

a. *Bad* means offensive, sorry, wicked, or ill; *badly* means in a bad manner.

> She feels *bad.* (ill)
> He behaved *badly.* (in an offensive manner)

b. Use *a* before consonants or consonant sounds; *an* before vowels or vowel sounds.

> He would like *an* (not *a*) egg for breakfast.
> *A* (not *an*) history book made good reading for *an* (not *a*) hour.
> *A* (not *an*) one-sided argument has little value.
> An inch is *a* (not *an*) unit of measure.

c. *Real* is an adjective of quality, while *very* is an adverb of degree. Use *real* to modify a noun, *very* to modify an adjective or an adverb.

> He is a violinist of *real* skill.
> You were *very* (not *real*) cold before you came inside.

    d. *Healthy* applies to people, *healthful* to things.

> The islanders are *healthy* (not *healthful*) people since they live on *healthful* (not *healthy*) foods.

    e. *This* or *that* means one kind or one object; *these* or *those* means more than one kind or object.

> They offer *this* (not *these*) kind of service.
> Tourists may choose from *these* (not *this*) kinds of souvenirs.
> *Those* students (not *them*) have completed the course. (*Them* never modifies.)

    f. *Then* has reference to time; *than* is used when making comparisons.

> The meal will be served *then* (not *than*) rather *than* (not *then*) later.

    g. *Better than* is used in comparing two items; *best* means "best of all."

> The book is *better than* the play. (Compare book and play)
> This is the *best* play in town. (Comparing all plays in town)

    h. Some words represent the ultimate degree. Comparisons can be made, however, if the word expresses an approach to the ultimate degree.

> That is *perfect*. (without fault)
> This is *more nearly perfect*. (approaching perfection)
> She owns a *unique* painting. (only one of its kind)

4. Choosing the wrong preposition is another common source of errors.

    a. *At* refers to a location in a smaller place; *in* implies *within,* such as within the boundaries of a larger city.

> His sister works *at* (not *in*) Kresge's.
> They now live *in* (not *at*) Cleveland.

    b. Use *among* with reference to three or more; *between* when only two persons or things are concerned.

> The candy was divided *among* (not *between*) the five children.
> The instructors decided *between* (not *among*) the two books.

    c. *Differ with* refers to opinion; *differ from* refers to things or persons.

> I *differ with* him on the basic approach to the problem.
> The new model *differs from* the old model in several ways.

    d. *As,* a conjunction, introduces or connects clauses; *like* functions as a verb or preposition.

> He acts *as if* (not *like*) he were hungry.
> He looks *like* (not *as*) his father.

Punctuation

Punctuation makes the meaning of the sentence clear, helps the reader understand the thought more easily and precisely, and assists one who is reading aloud to phrase and emphasize correctly.

The secretary who transcribes shorthand or machine dictation must be able to punctuate correctly, since many executives do not dictate punctuation.

THE APOSTROPHE ⟨ **'** ⟩

8-1. Spacing with the Apostrophe

Do not space before or after the apostrophe within a word. If the apostrophe follows the word, space after (but not before) the apostrophe.

boy's coat   boys' coat

8-2. Formation of Possessive Forms

1. If a noun (singular or plural) does *not* end in *s*, form the possessive by adding *'s*.

SINGULAR	PLURAL
child's	children's
man's	men's

2. If a singular noun ends in *s*, add *'s* to form the possessive if the *s* is to be pronounced as an extra syllable. If a singular noun ending in *s* would be awkward to pronounce with an extra syllable, add only the apostrophe to form the possessive.

boss's	politeness'
waitress's	species'

3. If a plural noun ends in *s*, add only the apostrophe to form the possessive.

bosses'	refugees'
managers'	youngsters'

4. To form the possessive of a singular proper name of one syllable ending in *s*, add *'s* to form the possessive.

James's   Charles's

5. To form the possessive of a singular proper name of more than one syllable ending in *s*, add only the apostrophe to form the possessive.

Roberts'   Williams'

53

6. To form the possessive of a plural proper name ending in *s,* add only the apostrophe to form the possessive.

Henrys'	Jameses'
Johnsons'	Adamses'

7. To form the possessive of a singular abbreviation, add *'s.* To form the possessive of a plural abbreviation ending in *s,* add only the apostrophe.

William Meyer, Jr.'s	Cooper Bros.' new store
YWCA's	the Ph.D.s' dissertations

8. To form the possessive of a compound noun, add *'s* to the last word.

runner-up's   brother-in-law's

Note: If a compound noun is plural, it is better to avoid the possessive form by rewording the sentence.

homes of the brothers-in-law *not* brothers-in-law's homes

8-3. Kinds of Possession

1. To Show Individual Ownership. Use the possessive form with each name to show individual ownership.

Sarah's and Sue's grades	W. T. Worden, Sr.'s estate
Carter's & Wright's stores	Duke of Kent's yacht
John's and Mary's books	Richard Grant's opinion

2. To Show Joint Ownership. Use the possessive form with only the last name in a series of two or more nouns.

Carter & Wright's store	Hall & Lowden Co.'s sale
Carter & Wright's stores	Norton-Roberts' Emporium

Note: If this rule makes the sentence ambiguous, use the possessive form with each noun or reconstruct the sentence.

AMBIGUOUS

Tom Wilson and Chauncey Smith's book remained in the box. (Is Tom in the box?)

BOTH NOUNS IN POSSESSIVE FORM (Better)

Tom Wilson's and Chauncey Smith's book remained in the box.

SENTENCE RECONSTRUCTED (Best)

The book belonging to Tom Wilson and Chauncey Smith remained in the box.

3. To Show Separate Possession. Indicate separate possession by making possessive each noun in a series.

Tom's, Chauncey's, and William's books were in the box.

4. To Indicate Authorship.

Bromfield's novels   Emerson's essays

5. As a Source.

    sun's rays   moon's beams

8-4. Apostrophe in Nonpossessive Situations

1. **In the Past Tense and Participles of Coined Verbs and Symbols.** Use the apostrophe to form the past tense or the participle of a coined verb and a symbol.

    He OK'd the bill.   When OK'ing the bill, he found an error.

    He X'd out the last line.   When X'ing out one mistake, he made another.

2. **With Inanimate Objects.** Generally, it is better not to use the possessive form with inanimate objects. Expressions suggesting personification or pertaining to measure or time, however, may be stated in the possessive form.

    The cover of the book (*not* the book's cover)
    Virtue's reward (personification)
    A dollar's worth (measure)
    A month's voyage (time)
    30 days' extension (time)
    six weeks' pay (time)

3. **Kind.**

    boys' shoes   women's dresses

4. **In Billing, Tables, or Technical Writing.** The apostrophe may be used to identify feet or minutes. Quotation marks, then, indicate inches or seconds.

    The time was 3 minutes 42 seconds.
    The time was 3'42".
    The room is 27 feet 4 inches long.
    The room is 27'4" long.

5. **As Single Quotation Marks.** Use the apostrophe for single quotation marks.

    He remarked, "I have read the article 'Food for Thought.' "

6. **In Contractions and Omissions.** Use the apostrophe to form contractions and to indicate the omission of numbers.

    they're   they are
    didn't   did not
    doesn't   does not
    it's *or* 'tis   it is
    Class of '69   Class of 1969
    The year '70   The year 1970

    Note: A contraction is formed by placing an apostrophe at the point at which the letter is omitted. An omission of a number is indicated by placing an apostrophe at the point at which the number is omitted.

7. In Plural Form of Figures, Etc. Use the apostrophe to indicate the plural form of figures, letters, symbols, and words.

> The extra 9's make a difference.
> His name is spelled with two r's.
> Use #'s instead of *'s.
> The paragraph contains too many *the*'s.

Note 1: If a word already contains an apostrophe, add only an *s* to form the plural.

> The don'ts are more numerous than the do's.

Note 2: Market quotations are customarily typed without the use of the apostrophe.

> Interstate 4s are up again.

Note 3: The apostrophe may be omitted in the plural form of figures, letters, symbols, and words if the omission does not detract from the clarity of the expression.

> The extra 9s make a difference.
> The CPAs looked forward to the 1970s.
> Use #s instead of *s.
> The whys and wherefores are not explained clearly.

8. In Organization Names. Current usage favors the elimination of the apostrophe from the name of an organization.

> The Doctors Club   Akron Attorneys Committee
> Eastern Teachers Association Citizens Bank

Note: The apostrophe is sometimes retained in the possessive form of an irregular plural or of a singular name.

> Children's Corner   Harry's Carpet Company
> The Women's Store   Woman's Exchange Shop

THE ASTERISK

8-5. Spacing with the Asterisk

When an asterisk falls within a sentence, it is considered to be part of the word it follows; therefore, space after, but not before, the asterisk. An asterisk which precedes a footnote is followed by one space.

> The article by De Craene* gives the instructor the information that he needed.

> * Andrew De Craene, "Evaluate Your Business Curriculum," *The Balance Sheet,* Vol. LI, No. 3 (November, 1969), p. 106.

8-6. With Other Punctuation Marks

When the asterisk and some other mark of punctuation occur at the same point, the asterisk follows the other mark of punctuation.

> the article by Jones,*   on each page.*

8-7. Uses of the Asterisk

1. With Footnotes. Use the asterisk in short manuscripts to refer the reader to footnotes.

The base year* was a good one; the year in question was not.**

---

* 1959
** 1969

2. In Omissions. Use three asterisks on a line by themselves to indicate the omission of one or more paragraphs. The asterisks should be centered; they may be typed with no intervening space or may be separated by one or more spaces.

* * *

Note: See Sections 8:22 and 8:23, pages 69 and 70, for the use of asterisks as ellipses.

3. As Substitutes. Use asterisks as substitutes for words that are unprintable or in bad taste.

Howard then called Mr. Smith a ***.

THE BRACE

8-8. Uses of the Brace

1. As a Joining Device. The brace is used to join related matter. On the typewriter it is represented by the joining of two or more parentheses.

State of Wisconsin)
County of Milwaukee)

2. In Legal and Tabular Work. Although the brace is not considered a mark of punctuation, it has its place in legal and tabular work.

SPECIAL SALE ON SUITS

$$\left.\begin{matrix} 7492 \\ \text{Lots } 1895 \\ 3396 \end{matrix}\right\} \text{at } \$8.95 \qquad \left.\begin{matrix} 855 \\ \text{Lots } 625 \\ 730 \end{matrix}\right\} \text{at } \$3.98$$

BRACKETS

8-9. Drawing or Typing Brackets

1. Brackets, which are sometimes referred to as glorified parentheses, may be drawn by hand or typed. If they are to be drawn, leave a space, when typing the copy, at the point where each bracket will be used. Then, after you have removed the paper from the machine, insert the brackets in ink.

2. If brackets do not appear on keys on the keyboard, type them as directed at the top of page 58.

a. To type the left bracket, follow this procedure: diagonal; backspace; underline; roll cylinder back one line; underline.

b. To type the right bracket, follow this procedure: underline; diagonal; backspace; roll cylinder back one line; underline.

8-10. Uses of Brackets

1. For Explanations. Use brackets to enclose an explanation or a note.

[These data do not include those for the current year.—Editor.]

2. With Insertions. Use brackets to enclose an explanation or comments inserted by someone other than the speaker or the author quoted.

". . . He was a soldier still!" [Applause.]

3. With Parenthetical Expressions. Use brackets to enclose parenthetical expressions in material that is within parentheses.

(See *A Manual of Style* [10th ed.], p. 101.)

4. For Editorial Corrections. Use brackets to show an editorial correction.

The Chinese [Moravians] were responsible.

5. For Phonetic Transcripts. Use brackets to show phonetic transcripts.

rouge [roozh]

6. For Pointing Out Errors. Use brackets to call attention to an error in quoted material by inserting [sic] after the questionable word or passage.

. . . they are true [sic] delightful people, even though their dress and manner are unusual.

7. With Enclosures. Use brackets to enclose such expressions as *Continued on page 56.* These expressions should also be italicized.

[*To be concluded.*]

Note: This rule applies to printed material. In typewritten material, underlines indicate italicized words or phrases.

THE COLON ⫶

8-11. Spacing with the Colon

Space twice after the colon, but do not space before it. Exceptions are reference initials in a letter, literary references, proportions, and time of day.

JCK:rh 3:1 (proportion)
The Weekly News, 7:21 2:05 p.m.

8-12. With Other Punctuation Marks

With a Quotation Mark. When a colon is used at the end of a quotation, the colon is placed outside the quotation mark.

> This is my opinion of the article "Personnel Problems": it is excellent.

8-13. Uses of the Colon

1. After Introductory Statements. The colon is used to introduce an explanatory statement, that is, a statement that explains the statement immediately preceding the colon.

> He offered a flimsy excuse: his car would not start.

> **Note:** If the explanatory statement is merely to explain or support the statement before the colon, it begins with a lower-case letter. If the explanatory statement requires special emphasis (such as the statement of a formal principle or rule), the explanatory statement begins with a capital letter.

> He referred to the principle: Art is its own justification for being.

2. After an Introductory Clause Followed by a Series. Use a colon after an introductory clause that introduces a series that contains an illustration or an enlargement of the meaning expressed in the first clause.

> An outstanding business letter makes an artistic appeal: Its parts are attractively arranged; it is free from erasures; it is correct in every detail.

3. After Introductory Expressions. Use the colon after introductory expressions containing *as follows, the following, these,* and *thus* that precede enumerations.

> Thomas Wolfe's best-known books are as follows: *The Return of Buck Gavin, Look Homeward Angel,* and *Of Time and the River.*

4. Before Listed Items. The colon is used before items that are listed, whether they are listed as straight text material or are typed with one item on each line. Items may or may not be numbered.

> He packed the gear essential to his assignment: camera, flash unit, film, and tripod.

> These subjects are to be photographed:
>
> Covered bridge
> Spinning wheel
> Grist mill

> Three things must be planned:
>
> 1. Mode of transportation
> 2. Route
> 3. Time of departure

5. After the Salutation. Use the colon after the salutation when mixed punctuation is used in a letter.

Dear Mrs. Bradford: Gentlemen:

6. To Separate Reference Initials. Use the colon to separate reference initials when the initials of the dictator and the initials of the secretary are used.

MB:EL   RCK:dfc

Note: No space precedes or follows the colon in reference initials.

7. With Quotations. The colon may be used to introduce long or formal quotations.

He recited the entire paragraph: "Inasmuch as . . . ."
The foreman of the jury responded: "Guilty."

8. With Introductory Remarks. Use a colon after the introductory remark of a speaker.

Ladies and Gentlemen: Fellow Officers:

9. Between Hours and Minutes. The colon is used to separate hours and minutes.

8:15 a.m.   4:07 p.m.   10:30 p.m.

Note: No space precedes or follows the colon used between hours and minutes.

10. In Expressions of Proportions. The colon is used to express proportions.

The rear axle has a 2:1 ratio.

Note: No space precedes or follows the colon in the statement of proportions.

11. In Literary References. The colon is used in footnotes between the place of publication and the name of the publisher.

Robert R. Aurner and Paul S. Burtness, *Effective English for Business Communication* (6th ed.; Cincinnati: South-Western Publishing Co., 1970)

12. In Literary References. The colon may separate volume and page numbers in literary references.

The Weekly News, 7:21

Note: No space precedes or follows the colon used to separate volume and page numbers.

13. In Biblical Citations.

John 3:15   Proverbs 10:2

Note: No space precedes or follows the colon used in biblical citations.

8-14. Times Not to Use the Colon

When the colon is used to introduce an explanatory statement or an enumeration, the implication is that the colon stands *directly* before the introduction and the explanation. It is therefore *incorrect* to use the colon if an expression intervenes between the introduction and the explanation.

> The following additional conditions must exist if the text is to be successful; some time will be required to establish them.
> 1. At least .05 inches of rainfall during a period of twelve hours.
> 2. A temperature no higher than 78°.

> These are the tools that will be needed. The list is quite complete.
>
> | Hammer | Adjustable wrench |
> | Saw | Screwdriver |

THE COMMA

8-15. Spacing with the Comma

Space once after the comma used with words, but do not space before it. Within a number, do not space before or after the comma.

8-16. With Other Punctuation Marks

1. **With a Quotation Mark.** When a comma is used at the same point as a quotation mark, the comma is always placed inside the quotation mark.

    > "Let me have a week," he asked, "to come to a decision."

2. **With an Asterisk.** When a comma occurs at the same point as the asterisk, the comma precedes the asterisk.

    > the book by Townsend,*

8-17. Uses of the Comma

1. **In a Series with a Conjunction.** Use the comma to separate words, phrases, or clauses in a series with a conjunction.

    > Desks, chairs, and cabinets were ordered in the same style.
    > The salesmen on the road, the men in the office, and the workers in the plant are all required to take this training.
    > The investigator found that the secretary was competent, that she worked steadily, and that she was familiar with all the operations of the office.

    Note: When *and, or,* or *nor* precedes the last element in the series, the comma should be inserted before the conjunction.

    > Red, and blue, and black, and white purses have been received. (four types)
    > Red, and blue, and black and white purses have been received. (three types)

2. In a Series Without a Conjunction. Use the comma after each word in a series when the conjunction has been omitted.

> Rain, snow, sleet, hail, were encountered during the trip.

3. With Pairs in a Series. Use the comma to separate pairs in a series or in a combination of expressions.

> The subject of his talk was "Sun and Sky, Moon and Stars, and Time and Tide."

4. In a Firm Name. Use commas to separate individual parts of a firm name and to precede *Inc.* Within a sentence, a comma should follow *Inc.*

> Moore, Stilson, Fredericks, and Jones Company
> Jetways, Inc., is the company name.
>
> **Note 1:** Omit the comma before the ampersand.
>
> Lawrence, Crosse & Smith Company, Inc.
>
> **Note 2:** If a company adopts for its firm name a style which eliminates the comma or other punctuation, use the adopted style in referring to that company.
>
> Adams, Caldwell and Royal

5. After "etc." Use the comma before and after the abbreviation "etc." when this abbreviation is used to complete items in a series.

> Occupational fields, engineering, medicine, teaching, etc., were discussed.

6. Between Adjectives Preceding a Noun. Use the comma to separate two or more adjectives preceding a noun when an idea of the same rank is expressed.

> He is a careful, competent craftsman.
>
> **Note:** When the adjectives give a single impression or one complete idea, no comma is used.
>
> The large round ball was tossed across the court.

7. With Adjectives in Pairs and in Series. Use the comma to set off pairs or series of adjectives following a noun.

> The typist, fast and accurate, was hard at work.

8. In Direct Address. Use the comma to set off expressions of direct address.

> John, your pen is here.
> That, my friend, is the way it is.

9. With Parenthetical Expressions. Use the comma to set off parenthetical words, phrases, or clauses.

> In the first place, the price is too high.
> The accuracy of that statement is, I think, subject to question.

Note: Commas may be omitted from parenthetical expressions to avoid overpunctuation.

> The book with the yellow cover was therefore not considered.
> That is perhaps a mistake we shall regret.

10. With Nonrestrictive Clauses, Phrases, or Words in Apposition. A nonrestrictive clause, phrase, or appositive is one that may be removed from a sentence without destroying the meaning of the sentence. It should be set off with commas.

> The boy, *who had his hat in hand,* stood at the door. (nonrestrictive clause)
> The boy, *hat in hand,* stood at the door. (nonrestrictive phrase)
> His first book, *Financial Management,* is out of print. (nonrestrictive appositive)
> His youngest son, *John,* obtained a fine position. (nonrestrictive appositive)

Note: A restrictive clause, phrase, or appositive is one that must be retained to keep the meaning of the sentence. It should *not* be set off with commas.

> The man *who was elected* is ill. (restrictive clause)
> A man *of fine character* is needed here. (restrictive phrase)
> The word *emigrate* is often confused with the word *immigrate.* (restrictive appositives)
> He *himself* was responsible. (restrictive appositive)
> Richard *the Lionhearted* is the hero of many young boys. (restrictive appositive)

11. In Compound Sentences. Use the comma between the members of a compound sentence connected by the conjunctions *and, or, but, for,* or *whereas.*

> She will hold the lantern, and he will chop the wood.
> He will get the information, and she will type the report.

Note 1: The comma may be omitted if a compound sentence is very short.

> Tom runs and Bill jumps.

Note 2: The comma should not be used (1) to separate independent clauses not joined by a conjunction or (2) in a compound sentence when at least one of the independent clauses is subdivided by commas. A semicolon should be used.

> Look across the river; see the other side.
> He was interested in history, science, and mathematics; but he cared little for other subjects.

12. Before the Conjunction "but." Use the comma before the conjunction "but" in a compound sentence whether it is long or short.

> Take all the food you like, but eat all you take.
> Close the windows and raise the shades.

13. In Dates. Use the comma to separate the day (or month) from the year in dates.

> September 12, 19--   October, 19--
>
> **Note:** When the date (including the year) occurs within a sentence, most writers place a comma after the year.
>
> They arrived May 24, 19--, and departed May 27, 19--.

14. In Addresses. Use the comma to separate the name of the city from the name of the state in an address.

> Denver, Colorado 80202   Pittsburgh, PA 15213
>
> **Note:** When the city and state names occur within a sentence, place a comma after the state name.
>
> The convoy left Lexington, Kentucky, and proceeded north.

15. To Indicate Omitted Verbs. Use the comma to indicate the omission of a verb.

> Alabama produces cotton; Virginia, tobacco; Ohio, tomatoes.

16. With Contiguous Verbs. Use the comma between verbs when one verb follows another directly.

> When you fall, rise and try again.
> Whatever you do, do it well.

17. With Proper Names in Succession. Use the comma to separate a succession of proper names.

> Because of Andres, Charles will remain here.

18. With the Phrases "as well as" or "together with," etc. When an expression such as *as well as, together with,* etc., is used in the subject, separate it from the rest of the sentence with commas.

> The chair, as well as the table, is on order.
> The first platoon, together with the second, has been ordered to advance at dawn.
>
> **Note:** These expressions do not affect the number of the verb. If the subject is singular, the verb is singular; if the subject is plural, the verb is plural.
>
> The desk, as well as the cabinets, is on order.
> The desks, as well as the cabinet, are on order.

19. With Expressions Introduced by the Words "or," "like," or "such as." Use a comma to separate appositive expressions introduced by the words "or," "like," or "such as."

> Office style, or the procedure followed in a specific office, is determined by the administrative staff.
> Scientists in New York, like those in California, must confine their control of the weather to worry.
> Marginal word changes, such as Office Copy, Invoice, etc., may be requested.

20. With Contrasting Expressions. Use the comma to separate contrasting expressions.

The more he gets, the more he wants.

21. After the Complimentary Close. Use the comma after the complimentary close when mixed punctuation is used in a letter.

Sincerely,   Very truly yours,

22. With Transposed Elements. Use the comma to set off an introductory dependent clause (a clause beginning with *if, as, when, unless, while, because, since,* etc.).

If it rains, the game will be canceled.

23. With Introductory Participial Phrases. Use the comma to set off an introductory participial phrase.

Running quickly to the window, he threw back the curtain.

24. With Transposed Names. Use a comma when the units in a proper name are transposed.

Anderson, Roy L.   Bates, C. J.

25. With Personal Name Suffixes and Academic Degrees. A comma should precede such personal name suffixes as *Sr., Jr., III* (or *3d*). Academic degrees are treated in the same manner.

Ray Trent, Jr.   R. B. Jones, III
Oliver Carson, Sr.   Price T. Smith, Esq.
James R. Dawson, M.D.   Walter Harrod, B.S.

26. With Introductory Series of Prepositional Phrases. If a sentence begins with a series of prepositional phrases, use the comma to set off the series.

At the end of the book in Chapter 29 on page 347, the name of the murderer is finally revealed.

27. With Unrelated Numbers. Use the comma to separate two unrelated numbers.

In 1969, 417 new policies were written.
On May 31, 178 people attended the lecture.

28. In Numbers of Four or More Digits. Use a comma to separate thousands, millions, etc., in a number of four or more digits.

$4,378   72,986   2,453,007

Note: Omit the comma when writing serial, telephone, street, page, and paragraph numbers.

405-24-7099   Social Security (serial) number
PN416843T   Policy (serial) number
216-871-6698   Telephone number
4402 Third Street   Street number

29. In Direct Quotations. Use the comma to set off a direct quotation.

> Mr. Wilson said, "I must leave."
> Mr. Thompson said, "We will continue without a break."

> **Note:** Do not use the comma if the quotation fits naturally in the sentence without a break.

> Mr. Thompson said that we will continue "without a break."

30. With Absolute Phrases. Use the comma to set off an absolute phrase.

> Campbell and Bridges deserve their raises, each being a top man in his field.

31. With Introductory Expressions. Use the comma to set off such expressions as *yes, no,* or *well* at the beginning of a sentence.

> Yes, it is really true.
> Well, there are some reservations.

32. With Introductory Infinitive Phrases. Use a comma to set off an introductory infinitive phrase.

> To run the race well, he must stay in condition.

33. With Series of Infinitive and Prepositional Phrases. Use commas between series of lengthy prepositional or infinitive phrases.

> He was prepared to conduct the survey, to tabulate the questionnaires, and to report the results.

34. With Short Questions Added to Statements. Use the comma to separate a short question added to a statement.

> That is what you said, isn't it?
> That is the gist of the matter, don't you think?

35. With a Question Within a Sentence. If the question is longer or independent, or if additional emphasis is desired, the question may be initiated with a capital letter.

> The problem is, What shall we do with the remainder?

36. For Contrast. Use the comma to separate contrasting and opposing phrases.

> The man acted quickly, yet wisely.
> You should walk, not run, to the exit.

37. To Set off Mild Interjections. Use the comma to set off a mild interjection.

> Oh, I don't know.

38. To Introduce Examples, Lists, Explanations, Enumerations.
An expression, such as *for example* (e.g.), *that is* (i.e.), *namely,* or *for instance,* introducing examples, lists, explanations, or enumerations, should be preceded by a semicolon (or a colon) and followed by a comma.

> He was interested in precious metals; for instance, gold, silver, and platinum.
> He complained of pain in several parts of his body: namely, his legs, arms, and hands.

> **Note:** If the introductory expression (*for example, that is, etc.*) is part of a parenthetical expression, that expression should be set off with commas or dashes.

> The undisciplined athlete, for instance, one who smokes or keeps late hours, will not go far.
> The undisciplined athlete—for instance, one who smokes or keeps late hours—will not go far.

39. With Dependent Expressions. Use commas to set off a dependent expression that breaks the continuity of the sentence.

> The engine, without its distributor rotor, could not be started.

40. For Clarity. Use a comma to separate expressions that might be incorrectly joined by the reader.

> Since that, time has passed quickly.

THE DASH

8-18. Spacing with the Dash

The dash is typed by striking the hyphen key twice without spacing before, between, or after the hyphens. It may be typed at the end of a line, but not carried to the beginning of the next line.

8-19. With Other Punctuation Marks

1. At the End of a Sentence. When an expression set off with a dash falls at the end of a sentence, only one dash is required to set the expression off from the rest of the sentence. The regular closing punctuation mark (period, question mark, or exclamation mark) replaces the closing dash at the end of the sentence.

> That was a mistake--a bad one!

2. Within a Sentence. When an expression requiring a question mark or exclamation mark is set off with dashes within a sentence, the question mark or exclamation mark ending the expression is retained before the closing dash.

> A huge salmon--the largest ever caught!--was placed on the scale.
> Chancey Witherspoon--is that really his name?--was paged again.

8-20. Uses of the Dash

1. **Change in Thought.** Use the dash to indicate a sudden change in thought or an afterthought.

>   Let us discuss--but what's the use?--no one will benefit.

2. **Before Name of Person Quoted.** Use the dash before the name of a person or an authority from whom material is quoted.

>   . . . dedicate ourselves anew to the work for the betterment of mankind.
>   --Franklin D. Roosevelt

3. **Before a Summarizing Statement.** Use the dash before a statement that summarizes the copy that precedes it.

>   He lost his stock, his personal property, his real estate--all the accumulations of a lifetime.

4. **With an Independent Interpolation.** Use dashes to set off a clause that is an independent interpolation.

>   The typist--believe it or not--completed this work in five minutes.

5. **Before and After a Long Appositive.** Use dashes before and after a long appositive within a sentence.

>   The farmer, the factory worker, the professional man--Americans in every walk of life--purchased bonds to help the government.

6. **In Faltering Speech.** Use dashes to represent faltering speech, hesitancy, or stammering.

>   This--er--was her--er--brother.

7. **For Added Emphasis or Clarity.** Dashes may be used instead of commas for added emphasis or clarity.

>   All agencies to some extent--and our agency to the fullest--offer this service.
>   The teacher graded the papers of the top students--Henry, Alice, John, and Mary--before those of the other students.

8. **To Introduce an Example or Explanation.** The dash may be used instead of the semicolon to introduce an example or explanation.

>   He is consistent player--he has scored at least 12 points in every game this year.

9. **To Introduce a List.** The dash may be used instead of a colon to introduce a list, usually when no word introduces the list.

>   Our busy season lasts only three months--January, February, and March.

THE DIAGONAL /

8-21. Uses of the Diagonal

1. With Abbreviations, Symbols, etc. The diagonal is useful when typing certain abbreviations, symbols, and business terms.

B/L   C/o   n/30 $1.25/M

2. In the Expression "and/or." Use the diagonal with the expression "and/or" to indicate an interchange of ideas.

Mary and/or John may file the report. (Either one or both may file the report.)

3. Fractions Not on the Keyboard. Use the diagonal to construct fractions that are not on the keyboard. Space between whole numbers and fractions.

He tried size 6 7/8.
The container held 2 3/4 gallons.

Note: Do not mix fractions on the keyboard with constructed fractions in the same sentence.

He tried size 6 1/2 and then size 6 7/8.
not
He tried size 6½ and then size 6 7/8.

ELLIPSIS MARKS • • •

8-22. Ellipses Used to Indicate Omissions

Ellipsis marks are used to indicate the omission of a word or words from a quotation. Ellipses consist of three periods or three asterisks separated by spaces.

. . . allow time for a hobby.
You will work better . . . if you have the rest you require.

8-23. Spacing with Ellipsis Marks

1. To Indicate an Omission Within a Sentence. Three periods or asterisks, separated by spaces from one another and from the copy in the sentence, are used to indicate an omission within a sentence. All punctuation in the quoted copy is retained.

If there is a special need for such copy in a business-promotion letter, . . . adapt your copy to its special purpose.

If there is a special need . . . adapt your copy to its special purpose.

2. To Indicate an Omission at the End of a Sentence. If an omission occurs at the end of a sentence, the ellipsis marks are inserted before the punctuation ending the sentence.

> Do not try to be an advertising copywriter in preparing routine business letters and memos . . . ! Use a normal business style.

> Advertising copy is often written with a special flair . . . . You may adapt your copy to its special purpose.

> **Note:** The ellipsis marks precede the exclamation point in the first example and the ending period in the second example because the omissions occur before the ending punctuation marks of the sentences.

3. To Indicate an Omission at the Beginning of a Sentence. If the quotation begins with the first word of the copy quoted, no beginning ellipsis marks are necessary because nothing has been omitted at the beginning of the sentence.

> Advertising copy is often written with a special flair or in a certain style.

> . . . is often written with a special flair or in a certain style.

THE EXCLAMATION POINT

8-24. Spacing with the Exclamation Point

Space twice after an exclamation point at the end of a sentence. Space once after an exclamation point within a sentence. Do not space before an exclamation point.

8-25. With Other Punctuation Marks

With a Quotation Mark. When a quotation is an exclamation, place the exclamation mark within the quotation mark. When an entire sentence is an exclamation, place the exclamation mark outside the quotation mark.

> Hear him shout, "Get that ball!"
> Stop repeating indifferently, "I don't care"!

8-26. Uses of the Exclamation Point

1. For Strong Feeling or Emotion. Use the exclamation point after words or groups of words that express strong feeling or emotion.

> Save those papers!
> Let him go!
> Stop the press!

2. For Irony, Dissent, and Amusement. Use the exclamation point to express derision, irony, amusement, or dissent.

> Would you believe him!
> How he rambles on!

3. After Interjections. Use the exclamation point after *Ah, Oh,* and other interjections when the point of emphasis is the interjection. Otherwise place the exclamation point at the end of the sentence.

> Ah, what bargains they offer!
> Ah! what bargains they offer.
> Oh, why do you do that!
> Oh! what a view.

> **Note:** "O" (always capitalized) always precedes a noun in direct address. It is never followed by any punctuation mark.

> O Susan, look!
> O Lord, we beseech Thee!

4. For Increased Intensity. Use the exclamation point after each word or phrase that shows increased intensity.

> Fire! Fire! rang through the air.
> He shouted, "No! No!"

5. With a Single Exclamatory Word. A single exclamatory word may be treated as a sentence.

> Stop! The bridge is out.
> Wait! I'm coming.
> Listen! I hear a siren.

> **Note:** To indicate a mild exclamation, use a comma or a period.
> Well, I wouldn't worry.
> Stop. It's time for lunch.

THE HYPHEN

8-27. Spacing with the Hyphen

Do not space before or after the hyphen (except when separating a house number and a street number, as in 127 - 32d Street).

8-28. Uses of the Hyphen

1. In Compound Words. Use the hyphen in certain compound words. (See Unit 11, pages 109-112.)

2. In Word Division. Use the hyphen to indicate division of a word at the end of a line. (See Unit 12, page 113.)

3. In Series of Numbers. Use the hyphen to indicate a continuous series of numbers. The hyphen replaces the word *through*.

    pages 10-24   1969-72   Volumes 2-8   John 3:2-4

4. In Compound Numbers. Use the hyphen to join words representing compound numbers from 21 to 99.

    twenty-one   one hundred sixty-seven
    ninety-nine   three thousand four hundred eighty-seven

5. With Certain Prefixes. Use the hyphen to join certain prefixes to words:

HYPHEN	NO HYPHEN
ex-president	cooperate
vice-president	preview
self-propelled	review

Note: Use the hyphen to join a prefix to a proper name.

    un-American   ex-Canadian   pro-Mexican

6. For Clarity. Use the hyphen to clarify otherwise ambiguous expressions.

    Harry is a junior college student. (ambiguous)
    Harry is a junior-college student. (clear)
    Harry is a junior college-student. (clear)

7. In Compound Adjectives. A hyphen may be used between two or more words serving as a single adjective before a noun.

    well-known author   small-scale model

Note 1: If the first word of the compound is an adverb that ends in *ly*, no hyphen is used.

    highly paid executive   poorly planned project

Note 2: Other instances in which a hyphen is not required in a compound adjective are given in Rule 11-2, pages 111 and 112.

8. With Compound Words Having a Common Base. When two or more compound words having a common base are used together, the base may be omitted in each word except the final one. In this case, all the hyphens are retained.

    The interim officers were elected to one-, two-, and three-year terms.

PARENTHESES

8-29. Spacing with the Parentheses

Do not space after the left parenthesis; do not space before the right parenthesis.

8-30. With Other Punctuation Marks

1. With a Period. When a parenthetical expression falls at the end of a sentence, the closing parenthesis does not enclose the period.

> Please order the usual size (small).
> The price of the item is too high ($19.95).

> **Note:** A period is not used within the parenthetical expression except after an abbreviation or when the parenthetical expression stands alone.

> Please send the package in the usual way (C.O.D.).
> That machine (it is described on page 29) is too big.
> The machine is described fully in this book. (See page 29.)

2. With a Question Mark. When the parenthetical expression—but not the entire sentence—is a question, the question mark is enclosed by the closing parenthesis; the period is not.

> John Wilson was the tallest boy in the class (or was it James Wilson?).

> **Note:** If the entire sentence is a question, the closing parenthesis does not enclose the question mark.

> Will you arrive the following day (January 21)?

3. With an Exclamation Point. When the parenthetical expression—but not the entire sentence—is an exclamation, the exclamation point is enclosed by the closing parenthesis; the period is not.

> James Wilson was the tallest boy in the class (not John Wilson!).

> **Note:** If the entire sentence is an exclamation, the closing parenthesis does not enclose the exclamation point.

> I must leave the following day (January 21)!

4. With a Comma, Semicolon, or Colon. A comma, semicolon, or colon is never used before the opening parenthesis. When a comma, semicolon, or colon is required *after* a parenthetical expression, the comma, semicolon, or colon is placed *after* the closing parenthesis.

> If you arrive early (7:00 a.m.), you may get a seat.
> The bill was sent promptly (March 22); however, no payment has been received.
> Read this menu (I have already read it): bacon, eggs, toast, and coffee.
> He ordered the following items (they are not needed immediately): pens, erasers, bond paper, and envelopes.

5. Complete Sentences as Parenthetical Expressions. When a complete parenthetical sentence stands alone after another sentence—whether the parenthetical sentence closes with a period, a question mark, or an exclamation point—the closing parenthesis encloses the final mark of punctuation.

> He did not attempt to defend his position. (He could not.)
> He did not attempt to defend his position. (How could he?)
> He did not attempt to defend his position. (He could not!)

8-31. Uses of the Parentheses

1. With Parenthetical Expressions. Expressions which are neither grammatically nor logically essential to the main thought of the sentence may be enclosed in parentheses. Such parenthetical expressions may range in length from a single word to several sentences.

> She examined the dress (size 12) for defects.
> The report is quoted in full. (See page 27.)
> First, he read from the book. (This is the same book mentioned on page 23. It is a handwritten record of the captain's voyages.) Next, he observed carefully the expression on the suspect's face.

Note 1: When parentheses appear within the body of a sentence, whatever other punctuation is necessary should be placed outside the closing parenthesis.

> If you want a smart picnic kit (this includes cooking utensils and space for food), investigate the ingenious combinations put out by Zenos.

Note 2: Commas or dashes should be used when the explanatory expression is more closely related to the main thought.

> He waved the cape, a red one, at the bull.
> He fell—feet first—down the chute.

2. With References. References to a source or an authority may be indicated parenthetically.

> The magazine listed (see page 106) the stores carrying the merchandise advertised.
>
> The crime rate in the city is up this year (*City News,* April 2, 19--).

3. With Periods of Time. Enclose in parentheses dates indicating a period of time.

> William Shakespear (1564-1616)

4. With Enumerations. Enumerated items within a sentence may be indicated by enclosing numbers or letters in parentheses.

> To enroll, you must (1) submit an application form, (2) give two personal references, (3) pass the admissions test, and (4) be interviewed.

5. With Dollar Amounts. In legal and business documents, when dollar amounts must be stated with extreme clarity and accuracy, the amount may be spelled out *and* typed in numbers enclosed in parentheses.

> the sum of Two Hundred (200) Dollars.
> the sum of Two Hundred Dollars ($200).

6. In Outlines. Use parentheses to enclose figures or letters used in outlines after the Roman numerals, capital letters, Arabic numbers, and lower-case letters have been exhausted. No period follows the parentheses. (Refer to page 77 for an illustration of this form.)

THE PERIOD

8-32. Spacing with the Period

Space twice after a period at the end of a sentence. Space once after the period at the end of an abbreviation within a sentence, but do not space after a period within an abbreviation. Do not space after a period used as a decimal point in a number.

> . . . was sent C.O.D. on May 5. The charge of $9.75 was paid.

8-33. With Other Punctuation Marks

1. With a Quotation Mark. When a quotation mark appears with a period, the period always precedes the quotation mark.

> The manager answered, "The shipment has not yet arrived."

2. With an Asterisk. When a period occurs at the same point as the asterisk, the period precedes the asterisk.

> the book by Garrison.*

8-34. Uses of the Period

1. At the End of a Sentence. Use the period at the close of a statement of fact.

> The company had a very successful year.

2. At the End of an Imperative Sentence. Use the period at the close of an imperative sentence or command.

> Make up a full report about the incident.

> **Note:** Some writers use condensed or telescoped expressions—sentences from which nonessential words have been eliminated. Such a telescoped expression should be followed by a period.

> Now, to the heart of the matter.
> Should we proceed? Perhaps.

3. At the End of a Request Statement. Use the period at the close of a request statement that begins with "Will you" or "May we."

> Will you please mail this letter immediately.
> May we have a copy of your annual report.

4. After Abbreviations and Initials. Use the period after an abbreviation and after an initial. If an abbreviation consists of two or more letters, each standing for a different word or words, use a period after each letter.

f.o.b.   C.O.D.   U.S.A.   Ph.D.   D.C.   Mich.
Mrs. C. R. Jones   R. D. Carlson   John S. Crawford

Note: Abbreviations composed of several capital letters are often written without periods.

AFT (American Federation of Teachers)
NEA (National Education Association)
FDIC (Federal Deposit Insurance Corporation)

5. Between Dollars and Cents and in Other Decimal Expressions. Use the period to separate dollars and cents written in figures. No space is left after the period.

$19.76 $250.50 $1,291.62

6. In Decimal Fractions. Use the period to separate the whole number from the fraction in a decimal. No space is left after the period.

12.76 percent   4.5 feet   10.75   9.875

7. In Timetables. Use the period to separate the hours from the minutes in timetables.

Leave Cincinnati   12.05 PM
Arrive Cleveland   12.55 PM

Note: In some timetables a colon is used between the hours and minutes. Also, "AM" and "PM" are sometimes listed as "a" and "p."

8. After Run-in Headings. Use the period after a heading run into a paragraph.

Courtesy. Another of the positive qualities that an office worker should cultivate is courtesy.

9. In Ellipsis Marks. Use periods to type ellipsis marks to indicate an omission at the beginning of, within, or at the end of a sentence.

. . . report was encouraging and . . . we expect to attain even better results this year. . . .

Note: See Sections 8-22 and 8-23, pages 69 and 70, for the use of periods as ellipses.

10. With Detached Words or Phrases. Use the period at the close of detached words or phrases in modern style.

Yes, in answer to your statement.
Pity, for the loss of roses.
—Virginia Woolf

11. In Outlines. Use the period after the numbers and letters designating parts of an outline, unless such symbols are enclosed in parentheses.

```
I.  -------------------
    A.  -----------------------
    B.  -----------------------
        1.  --------------------
        2.  --------------------
        3.  --------------------
            a.  ----------------------
            b.  ----------------------
                (1)  -----------------
                (2)  -----------------
                    (a)  -----------------
                    (b)  -----------------
II.  -------------------
    A.  ---------------------
        1.  --------------------
        2.  --------------------
```

12. With an Indirect Question. Use a period at the end of an indirect question.

> He asked if the ship is in.
> The manager wanted to know if the letter had been written.

8-35. Times Not to Use the Period

1. After a Signature. See the letters illustrated on pages 26-32 for the correct form.

2. After Roman Numerals. See Rule 8-34:11, above, for an exception. See Rule 8-42:13, page 83, for use of Roman numerals.

3. After Titles, Display Lines, etc. Omit the period after a title, a display line, or a heading. The exception is a run-in heading of a paragraph.

4. In Enumerated Lists. Omit the period after items in enumerated lists.

> 13 Filing cabinets
> 12 Desks
> 12 Chairs
> 2 Telephone stands

5. After Identification Letters. Omit the period after a letter used to identify a person or a thing.

> Teacher B   Grade A   Mr. C   Plan D

6. After the Term "Percent." Omit the period after the term "percent."

> The cost of living increased 4.5 percent this past year.

7. After Chemical Symbols.

> NaCl is the symbol for sodium chloride (salt).

8. After Ordinals.

. . . letter was mailed on the 3d of June.
. . . is the 21st in terms of profitability.

9. In Contractions.

can't   mayn't   they'll   he'll   won't   didn't

10. In Abbreviations in Timetables and Tabulations.

AM	fob	doz
PM	COD	yds

11. After an Abbreviation at the End of a Sentence. Omit the period after an abbreviation that closes a sentence. The period at the end of the sentence serves both purposes.

The letter was addressed to North and Jones, Inc.
The goods were shipped C.O.D.
He works in the office of the Hayworth Metals Co.

Note: If the abbreviation is enclosed in parentheses, the additional period is required.

The amount is $25.20 (C.O.D.).

THE QUESTION MARK

8-36. Spacing with the Question Mark

Space twice after a question mark at the end of a sentence. Space once after a question mark within a sentence. Do not space before a question mark.

8-37. With Other Punctuation Marks

1. With Quotation Marks. When the sentence is a statement and the quotation is a question, the question mark lies inside the quote.

The presiding officer said, "Shall we pass this bill?"

Note: If the quotation begins a sentence and includes a question mark, no other punctuation is needed.
"Do you want to leave now?" he asked.

2. With Quotation Marks. When the sentence is a question and the quotation is a statement, the question mark lies outside the quote.

Has he approved your suggestion, "All changes must be in writing"?

3. With Quotation Marks. When both the sentence and the quotation are questions, the quote takes precedence and the question mark lies inside the quote.

Have you ever been approached with the question, "Shall I own my own home?"

4. With a Period Following an Abbreviation. If a question ends with an abbreviation ending in a period, the question mark follows the period.

> Shall I send the book C.O.D.?

8-38. Uses of the Question Mark

1. After a Direct Question. Use the question mark after every direct question.

> What is the correct time?
> Will you go?

2. With Interrogative Implication. Use the question mark when the implication is interrogative, even if the expression is formed as a statement.

> That was a long hike?
> You think this course of action to be wise?

3. To Indicate Uncertainty. The question mark may be used within parentheses to indicate uncertainty or doubt.

> He was born in 1926 (?).

4. With a Series of Questions. Each question within a sentence should be followed by a question mark.

> Do you think he is trustworthy? loyal? dependable?

5. With an Independent Question Within a Sentence. An independent question within a sentence is set off with a comma, begins with a capital letter, and terminates with a question mark.

> The question is, What was the score at the end of the first quarter?

> **Note:** When a short direct question follows a statement, use a comma before and a question mark after the question.

> He will score, won't he?

8-39. Times Not to Use the Question Mark

1. After an Indirect Question. Do not use the question mark after an indirect question.

> He asked whether we were coming or going.
> I asked them when the road had been repaired.

2. After a Polite Request. Do not use the question mark after a polite request, a suggestion, or an order, even if it is phrased as a question.

> Will you please close the door.
> Will you have the report on my desk by Friday.

QUOTATION MARKS   " "

8-40. Spacing with Quotation Marks

Space twice after the quotation mark at the end of a sentence; otherwise, space once before the opening quotation mark and once after the closing quotation mark.

8-41. With Other Punctuation Marks

1. With a Period. When an abbreviation or a sentence ends with a period, the period is always placed inside the closing quotation mark.

> The teller replied, "Your account is overdrawn."

2. With a Question Mark. If the sentence is a question and the quotation a statement, the question mark is placed outside the quotation mark.

> Did he say, "It is time to go"?

> **Note:** If the quoted material, as well as the sentence, is a question, only one question mark is required; and it is placed inside the quotation mark.

> Did he ask, "Is it time to go?"

3. With a Question Mark. If only the quoted material is a question, the question mark is placed inside the closing quotation mark.

> He asked, "Is it time to go?"

> **Note 1:** Whether the question mark is placed inside or outside the closing quotation mark, no period (or other additional mark of punctuation) is required to close the sentence.

> He replied, "Must I?"
> Did he reply, "Must I?"
> Did he reply, "I must"?

> **Note 2:** If the quotation begins a sentence and includes a question mark, no comma is needed.

> "Must I?" he replied.

4. With an Exclamation Mark. If the exclamation mark is part of the quotation, it is placed inside the closing quotation mark.

> She cried, "Help!"

> **Note 1:** If the exclamation mark is not part of the quotation, it is placed outside the closing quotation mark.

> That package must be marked "Fragile"!

> **Note 2:** Whether the exclamation mark is placed inside or outside the closing quotation mark, no period (or other additional mark of punctuation) is required to close the sentence.

> She screamed, "Help me!"
> She must answer, "Present"!

5. With a Comma. The comma is always placed within the closing quotation mark.

> "This is an important assignment," he said.

6. With Colons and Semicolons. Colons and semicolons are always placed outside the quotation marks.

> He called, "Run to the top of the hill"; he did not know the ambush was there.
> The following items were in the package marked "Fragile": a camera, two lenses, a tripod.

8-42. Uses of Quotation Marks

1. For Words Defined and Foreign Words. Words defined, unfamiliar foreign words, and translations of foreign words or expressions are enclosed in quotation marks. (It is also acceptable to underline unfamiliar foreign words instead of enclosing them in quotes.)

> "Marine" means "of or pertaining to the sea."
> The remark was made in "bonne foi."

Note: Foreign words need not be enclosed in quotation marks if they are so commonly used that they have become a part of the English language.

> The chateau was built high on the hill.
> The country prospered under that regime.

2. For Speeches and Writings. The exact words of a speaker or a writer are enclosed in quotation marks. A brief quotation is set off with a comma.

> He replied, "No, I can't go."
> "No, I can't go," he replied.

3. For Multiple-Sentence Quotations. If a quotation consists of more than one sentence of a single paragraph, the entire quotation is enclosed in one set of quotation marks.

> "The order was placed January 19. It has not been shipped."

4. For Multiple-Paragraph Quotations. If a quotation consists of more than one paragraph, quotation marks are used at the beginning of each paragraph and at the end of the last paragraph.

> "_____
> _____
> _____.
> "_____
> _____."

5. For Conversation and Dialogue. Each remark is introduced by paragraphing.

> "What do you think of the weather?" asked the tourist.
> "Miserable," said the farmer, turning to adjust the harness on his mule.
> "Is it always this bad?"
> "Only during the tourist season."

6. For Poetry. When poetry is quoted, a quotation mark is placed at the beginning of each stanza and at the end of the last stanza.

> "An arrow, flaming from the eastern sky
> To blaze in radiant arc, then fall, and die,
> Is quenched forever in the western sea
> and leaves a darkened world to wonder—Why?
>
> "The drama starts anew with rising sun;
> Its players know not how the plot should run.
> Bewildered actors play the mad charade—
> Before they learn their parts, the play is done."

7. As Ditto Marks. Use the quotation mark to type ditto marks.

> Take one green   pill at   9:00.
> "   "   blue   "   "   "
> "   "   orange "   "   10:00.

8. To Show Interrupted Quotations. Within a sentence, expressions which interrupt quotations (such as *she said, the author stated*) are set off with commas. Note that the continuation of the quotation does *not* begin with a capital letter.

> "The sun will shine," he said, "after the shower."

> **Note:** If the continuation commences at the beginning of a sentence, the continuation *does* begin with a capital.

> "The sun will shine again after the shower," he said. "It always has."

9. For Quotations Within Quotations. A quotation within a quotation is identified with single quotation marks (typed with the apostrophe key).

> He said, "I asked Mr. Henderson to go, but he said, 'No!' "

10. To Show Words as Words. In referring to a word itself rather than to the thing the word represents, enclose the word in quotation marks.

> He put "horse" on the chalkboard.

> **Note:** In printed material, the word is often italicized—not enclosed in quotation marks.

11. For Slang. Slang, ungrammatical expressions, and humorous or ironical expressions are sometimes enclosed in quotation marks. Many writers think, however, that the writer patronizes his reader by using quotation marks in this manner. Some who use quotation marks in this manner do so to imply an apology; others feel that if unorthodox form is the best means of expression, no apology is necessary.

> I "ain't" going.   I ain't going.
> It "weren't did" that way.   It weren't did that way.
> His "funny" story was not funny.   His funny story was not funny.

12. For Unusual or Technical Terms. Unusual or technical terms used in nontechnical writing (where the reader would not be expected to understand them) may be enclosed in quotation marks.

> He used an "RF generator" to complete the test.
> "Co-Mo" soap has become very popular.

13. For Parts of Books. The titles of subdivisions of books (chapters, units, lessons) are enclosed in quotation marks.

> Read Chapter IV, page 59, "Business Law and the Consumer."

> **Note 1:** The words and numbers which identify the major parts of the book (chapters, units) are capitalized but not placed within quotation marks.

> Read Chapter VIII for tomorrow.

> **Note 2:** Minor divisions of books (page, line) are not placed inside quotation marks.

> Please refer to page 23.

14. For Works of Literature and Art. Titles of the following items are usually enclosed in quotation marks:

Articles	Musical Compositions
Essays	Paintings
Lectures	Poems
Mottoes	Sculptures

> He referred to the article "How to Write Effectively."
> The subject of his talk was "Looking to Tomorrow."

8-43. Times Not to Use Quotation Marks

1. In Scripts. In scripts and court testimony, each speaker is identified; quotation marks are unnecessary.

> Sally: Did you go out with George last night?
> Sue: Yes, I did.
> Sally: Did you have a good time?
> Sue: Oh, yes!

2. For Long Quotations. If a quotation consists of four or more typewritten lines, the quotation may be introduced by a colon and typed with single spacing on a line shorter than the standard line used for the page. In this case, quotation marks are not used.

> Although the question is still subject to some dispute by other authorities, Johnson says:
>
> > It must be remembered that the child's early environment is of paramount importance in the formation of attitudes toward school and study. If, at home, he has observed a lack of respect for authority, it is to be expected that he will not respect school authorities.[1]

> **Note:** The colon following the introductory statement is sometimes omitted.

3. For Well-Known Phrases. Do not use quotation marks to enclose well-known phrases.

> He really believes that a stitch in time saves nine.

4. For Indirect Quotations. Do not use quotation marks to enclose indirect quotations.

> He said that he could not go.
> Mr. Anderson said that he reads the magazine.

THE SEMICOLON

8-44. Spacing with the Semicolon

Space once after the semicolon; do not space before the semicolon.

8-45. With Other Punctuation Marks

With a Quotation Mark. When a semicolon is used at the end of a quotation, the semicolon is placed outside the quotation mark.

> The chairman said, "The meeting is adjourned"; the members prepared to leave.

8-46. Uses of the Semicolon

1. To Replace a Conjunction. A semicolon should be used to separate independent clauses of a compound sentence when a conjunction (*and, but,* or *nor*) is omitted.

> He took a long walk, but the exercise failed to relax him. (conjunction)
> He took a long walk; the exercise failed to relax him. (semicolon)

> **Note:** In a short compound sentence, no internal punctuation is necessary, unless the conjunction *but* is used.

> He walked and I ran.
> He walked, but I ran.

2. In a Compound Sentence. If either clause in a compound sentence contains one or more commas, a semicolon is used before the conjunction.

> He took a long, brisk walk; but the exercise failed to relax him.

3. Between Items in a Series. When one or more items in a series contain a comma, the semicolon is used to separate the items. The semicolon in this case is used as a "super comma" that will not be confused with commas within the items.

> The names listed were: Willis, James; Jones, Thomas; Wright, Henry; and Jefferson, Andrew.

4. Before a Conjunctive Adverb or Transitional Phrase. Use a semicolon before a conjunctive adverb or transitional phrase between two independent clauses.

Examples of conjunctive adverbs and transitional phrases are: accordingly, consequently, furthermore, hence, however, in addition to, in fact, likewise, moreover, nevertheless, notwithstanding, otherwise, so, still, when, therefore, thus, yet.

> The presumptions are reasonable and the logic is sound; therefore, we must accept the conclusion.

5. To Introduce an Illustration or a Series. A semicolon should precede a word or an abbreviation used to introduce an illustration that is a complete clause or to introduce a series that is made up of several items.

> Ralph Jameson is the chief officer; that is, he has the final responsibility.
> His travels took him to many nations; for example, Spain, Switzerland, and England.
> A profitable business benefits many; i.e., its owners, its customers, and other industries.

6. After Clauses Following a Colon. Use a semicolon to separate a series of clauses immediately following a colon.

> The automobile is an important machine: It is a means of transportation; it is a source of pleasure; it is an important generator of economic activity.

7. Comparisons with Use of Comma and Conjunctive Adverbs.

a. Conjunctions (*and, but,* or *nor*) connect independent clauses smoothly.

> She is very stout, but she is rich.

b. Substituting a semicolon for the conjunction emphasizes the separate nature of the elements of the sentence.

> She is very stout; she is rich.

c. The separateness of the elements can be emphasized even more strongly by using a conjunctive adverb.

> She is very stout; however, she is rich.

> **Note:** Some other conjunctive adverbs are: moreover, consequently, nevertheless, otherwise, therefore, accordingly, hence, still, thus, so, yet.

d. Although a semicolon always precedes a conjunctive adverb, the comma which *may* follow it is optional, depending on the emphasis desired. The comma is more often omitted after common one-syllable conjunctive adverbs.

> He was rather weary; yet he was determined to go.
> He had not prepared for a rainy day; consequently, he was soaked to the skin.

THE UNDERLINE

8-47. With Other Punctuation Marks

The underline is not used below punctuation marks that immediately precede or follow a continuously underlined section. Punctuation marks within a continuously underlined section *are* underlined.

> Angela purchased six tickets for the evening performance of Two Days' Journey into Fear.
> He read Abbott's latest book, Men, Machines, and Skills.

8-48. How to Type the Underline

The underline is typed solid, including the space between words, in titles. In other instances, each word may be underlined separately if the intent is to emphasize each word separately.

> She read another chapter of The Blue Sky.
> Please walk rapidly to the end of the bridge.

> **Note:** General current practice is to use a continuous underline in all instances, unless the intent is to call special attention to each word.

8-49. Uses of the Underline

1. **As a Mark of Punctuation.** The underline is considered a mark of punctuation and should replace the frequent use of quotation marks in typing. A profusion of quotation marks gives the typewritten page an unbusinesslike "lacy" appearance.

2. **For Titles of Publications.** The continuous underline should be used to identify titles of books, magazines, newspapers, and music. Another permissible style, to be used for special emphasis in typing titles of books, is to use all capital letters.

   > The book is entitled How I Found Peace.
   > The book is entitled HOW I FOUND PEACE.
   > He subscribed to the magazine Sports Illustrated.
   > The advertisement appeared in the December 2 issue of the Plain Dealer.

3. **For Works of Art, Emphasis, and Words under Discussion.** Use the underline for titles of work of art, for emphasis, and to set off any words or phrases under discussion.

   > The critics reviewed Escape.
   > Please rush it to the printer.
   > Confine your remarks to relevance.

4. **To Indicate Italics.** Use the underline to indicate to the printer any words or phrases that are to be italicized when set in type. (See Unit 20, page 173.)

Capitalization

Most capitalization is based on convention, but capitalization is sanctioned by business also as a device for securing emphasis. Proper capitalization also aids in clarifying ideas. Frequently the omission of a capital letter that is needed changes the meaning of the sentence. The same words may be capitalized in one instance and not in another, the choice being contingent on the thought to be expressed.

9-1. Academic Degrees. Capitalize the abbreviations of academic degrees, but not the names of the degrees when combined with the word *degree*.

B.S.	a bachelor of science degree
M.S.	a master of science degree
B.A. in Ed.	Bachelor of Arts in Education

9-2. Academic Fields. Capitalize each principal word in the name of a specific course of study, but not the name of a field of study.

Ancient History I	ancient history course
Thermodynamics 202	thermodynamic studies
Algebra II	algebra test

9-3. Advertising Material and Trademarks. In advertising material, words to be emphasized are often capitalized. Trademarks are usually capitalized even in general usage.

We recommend the Large Economy Size.
Ivory Soap   Delicious apples   Timex watches

9-4. Astronomical Bodies. Capitalize the names of astronomical bodies, except the words *earth, moon, sun, star*.

Jupiter	Milky Way
Mars	Ursa Major

Note: When *earth, moon,* and *sun* are used with the names of other astronomical bodies, they, too, are capitalized.

He discussed the relationship of Mars, Jupiter, the Moon, and Earth.

9-5. Books, Booklets, Newspapers, Magazines, and Theses. Titles of books, booklets, newspapers, magazines, and theses may be (1) typed in all capital letters or (2) underlined with the first letters of the principal words capitalized. (Articles, conjunctions, and short prepositions [four letters or less] are not capitalized unless such a term is used as the first word.)

BUSINESS ENGLISH (book)
THE CINCINNATI ENQUIRER (newspaper)
POPULAR PHOTOGRAPHY (magazine)
A STUDY OF PROFIT-SHARING PLANS (thesis)

Business English (book)

The Cincinnati Enquirer (newspaper)

Popular Photography (magazine)

A Study of Profit-Sharing Plans (thesis)

Note: Some style guides recommend that prepositions of four letters be capitalized. Each office should establish which rule (capitalizing a preposition of four or a preposition of five letters) should be followed.

9-6. Business Products. If the name of a business product refers to one specific product rather than to a class of products, and if that name is a trademark, the name is treated as a proper name and is capitalized. Ordinarily only the trademark is capitalized and not a following descriptive word unless the descriptive word is part of the trademark.

Minute Maid	Green Giant
Palmolive soap	Bab-O
Bon Ami cleanser	Cream of Wheat

Esser Castile Soap, but a bar of castile soap

Note: The name of a market grade is sometimes capitalized.

Choice beef (market grade)   Prime beef (market grade)

9-7. Compound Words. Capitalize the individual parts of a compound word in a title or in a heading just as they would be capitalized if the hyphen were omitted. In text copy, only the proper noun or proper adjective in a compound word is capitalized.

Day-to-Day Health Care (title)
Sixty-Second Diner (title)
They visited the French-speaking part of Canada.
The American-made product was a success.

9-8. The Deity (or References to), Books and Divisions of the Bible, Holy Days, and Creeds. Capitalize words referring to the Deity, the Bible, holy days, and creeds.

God	Easter
Psalms	Apostles' Creed
Genesis	Savior

Note 1: Adjectives derived from the Bible are written with small letters.

apocryphal   biblical   scriptural

Note 2: The word *bible* is not capitalized when it is used allegorically.

That handbook is my bible.

9-9. Directions. The directions *north, south, east,* and *west* are capitalized when they refer to definite sections of the country or are used with other proper names.

the East Side	the eastern half of the lot
rivers of the West	the east side of the road
North America	the western border
415 South Fifth Street	the north half
Northern Ontario	south of Suez

9-10. Formal Writings. Any statement which follows the word RESOLVED or the word WHEREAS is indicative of formal writing. The statement should begin with a capital letter.

RESOLVED, That the purpose of this organization . . . .
WHEREAS, The aforementioned party . . . .

9-11. Geographic Terms. Proper names that are geographic terms begin with capital letters.

the Ohio River	Coral Lake
Hamilton County	Atlantic Ocean
Wisconsin Avenue	Yellowstone National Park
the Rocky Mountains	San Francisco

Note 1: If reference is made to two or more geographic entities of the same nature, the common plural designation may or may not be capitalized. In business writing, the common noun following two or more proper geographic terms is usually not capitalized; but the United States Government Printing Office *Style Manual* and certain other style guides recommend capitalization.

the Ohio and Missouri rivers *or* the Ohio and Missouri Rivers
Coral and Echo lakes *or* Coral and Echo Lakes

Note 2: A descriptive word preceding the proper name of a geographic term is not capitalized.

the river Nile	the city of Pittsburgh
the state of Indiana	the country of Brazil

Note 3: Nicknames referring to places are capitalized.

the Bluegrass State (Kentucky)	the Lone Star State (Texas)
the Queen City (Cincinnati)	the Ditch (the Panama Canal)

Note 4: Words derived from the names of places are not capitalized when the words have developed specialized business meanings.

plaster of paris	china
french sleeve	anglicize
dutch cut	bohemian

9-12. Government Terms. Government terms, such as *constitution, federal, government,* and *national,* when used as part of a title or when used as adjectives referring to a specific government are capitalized. These terms should not be capitalized, however, in general use.

> In case of conflict between the state constitution and the Federal Constitution, the latter prevails.
> It is within the power of Congress to protect the Government of the United States from armed rebellion.
> The government agents are scheduled to visit three national banks this afternoon.
>
> **Note:** In many publications today, there is a trend toward not capitalizing government terms when they are used as adjectives or when they refer to a specific government.
>
> As a result of federal legislation passed in 1913, our Federal Reserve Banking System was created.
> To perform its functions, the government spends money and obtains the money it needs from the people.

9-13. Historical Periods, Wars, and Holidays. Names designating historical periods, wars, and holidays are proper names and should be capitalized.

> Colonial Period   Stone Age
> World War II   Civil War
> Fourth of July   Memorial Day
> Christmas   Labor Day

9-14. Institutions. The names of churches, schools, libraries, government agencies, and other institutions of a public character begin with capital letters.

> Asbury Methodist Church, *but* a local Methodist church
> Central High School, *but* a school in a central location
> Fairmont Public Library, *but* a public library in Fairmont
> Detroit Public Health Department, *but* a public health agency
>
> **Note 1:** In the names of institutions, capitalize *the* only if this word is part of the official name of the institution.
>
> The student applied for admission to The College of Steubenville.
> The alumnus sent a contribution to The University of Texas.
>
> **Note 2:** When the full name of an institution is well known or has already been established, a single brief word can be used to identify the institution. The key word should be capitalized.
>
> At the request of the members of the Board of Education, the Superintendent sent a copy of the report to each member of the Board.
> After the President addressed the key personnel of the Department of Defense, he sent his personal greetings to all the employees of the Department.

9-15. Letters. There are set rules for capitalization in the typing or writing the various parts of business letters.

Attention line: Capitalize the first word and all the principal
                         words.

Salutation: Capitalize the first word and all nouns.

Subject line: Capitalize the first word and all the principal
                         words.

Complimentary close: Capitalize only the first word.

Attention Director of Personnel   Subject: Notice of Approval
Attention Sales Department   Subject: End-of-Month Sale
Attention Mr. James Furst
                                      Very truly yours
Dear Friend   Yours very truly
My dear Madam   Cordially
Dear Mrs. Johnson
To all Associates
To the Heads of all Departments

Note: In attention lines, special salutations, and subject lines,
the conventions described above may be altered to achieve
special emphasis or special effects.

Attention ALL PERSONNEL   SUBJECT: Special Sale of
                                       Coats
To All Associates   SPECIAL SALE OF COATS
To THE HEADS OF ALL
   DEPARTMENTS

9-16. Names of Individuals. Capitalize the first letter of each name and the
nickname of a person.

Maurice T. Martin   Mr. Music Man
Sharon Helfenstein   Red Jones
Old Hickory   Curly Dickson
Stonewall Jackson   Joe Sawyer

Note 1: Capitalize the name of a person exactly as the person
himself capitalizes it.

Louis E. de la Porte   Jeanne van Dever
George VanDeRyt   Timothy O'Toole

Note 2: Do not capitalize certain words with special meanings
derived from proper names.

chinaware   pasteurize
macademize   platonic

9-17. Nouns with Numbers. Most nouns preceding a figure are capitalized
in business writing, including job instructions. Common nouns, such
as *page, line, sentence,* and *paragraph,* may be typed with or without
the capital when these nouns precede a figure.

Room 27   Line 27
Section 21   Lesson 9
Chapter IX   Unit 12
Sentence 3   page 10

9-18. Organizations. Capitalize each principal word in the name of an association, club, foundation, business firm, radio and television station, etc.

> the Ohio Association of Technical Institutes
> The Happy Boys Club
> the Horace Green Foundation
> Henderson Dry Cleaners
> Radio Station WKRC
> Television Station WLW-T

> **Note:** Common nouns should be capitalized when they stand for proper names. The full proper name should be stated in full the first time it is used in a document; it will then be understood that subsequent use of the shorter form refers to the full name. (See Rule 9-14, Note 2, also.)

> The Bank of America is that institution. The Bank . . . .
> The Board of Regents will rule on the question. The Regents . . . .

9-19. Outlines. Each section of an outline begins with a capital letter.

> I. OUTLINE OF POWERS

>> A. Powers of the Senate
>>> 1. To confirm certain appointees
>>> 2. To ratify treaties
>>> 3. To try impeachments

> **Note:** Refer to page 181 for another acceptable style of capitalizing the words in an outline.

9-20. Personal Titles. Capitalize every principal word in a title that refers to a specific person. A title not referring to a specific person is not capitalized unless it is a title of high distinction.

> The present Secretary of the Treasury is on vacation.
> The presidents of several organizations were present.
> The President of the United States faces grave responsibilities.
> President Grant was a colorful president.

> **Note 1:** All titles in addresses and closing line of business letters should be capitalized.

IN INSIDE ADDRESS	IN CLOSING LINES
Mr. J. H. Andrews, Sales Manager	Lawrence C. Smith, Manager
Mr. Peter Dunlap, President	Richard Towns, Editor

> **Note 2:** The titles of all officers are capitalized in constitutions, bylaws, and the minutes of meetings of organizations.

> The meeting was adjourned by the Chairman.

9-21. Plays. The title of a play may be (1) typed in all capital letters, (2) underlined with the principal words capitalized, or (3) enclosed in quotation marks with the principal words capitalized.

> THE IMPORTANCE OF BEING EARNEST
> The Importance of Being Earnest
> "The Importance of Being Earnest"

9-22. Poetry. Capitalize the first word of each line of poetry unless the author chooses to use lower-case letters.

> A gentle mist rolls in at eventide
> Creating shadow worlds where one may hide
> To seek the image of his own desire
> And cast the torment of the day aside.
>
> And overhead
> the sympathetic finch
> chirps and thrills
> approval.
>
> —John Dos Passos

9-23. Prefixes. When a prefix is added to a word which should be capitalized, the prefix begins with a lower-case letter.

> non-European un-American
> trans-Asiatic pre-Revolutionary

9-24. Proper Names of Things. Names of businesses, buildings, hotels, rooms, vehicles, etc., begin with capital letters.

> Suburban Dry Cleaners Room 342
> Central Building Oldsmobile
> Henderson Hotel Mack Truck
> Caprice Room Plymouth

9-25. Questions. Begin with a capital letter an independent question that begins within a sentence. (The question is preceded by a comma.)

> I am confronted with the question, Should I own my own home?

Note 1: The question mark can replace the comma within a sentence if the question begins the sentence.

> Should I own my own home? is the question.

Note 2: When a sentence contains a series of brief questions, which themselves are not complete sentences, begin each question with a lower-case letter.

> Is the plan complete? prudent? feasible?

9-26. Quotations. Capitalize the first word of a quotation unless it is (1) a fragmentary quotation or (2) an interrupted quotation resumed within a sentence.

> The captain said, "We will take the hill."
> The captain said his company would "take the hill."
> "We will take the hill," the captain said, "if artillery support is available."

9-27. Races, Nationalities, Languages, Religions. Capitalize the names of races, nationalities, languages, and religions.

> Negro Caucasian
> Canadian English
> French Hebrew
> Methodist Presbyterian

9-28. Relatives. Capitalize a word which designates family relationship *unless* it is preceded by a pronoun.

> I told Father about it.
> He saw Uncle Will.
> He wrote to Grandfather Smith.
> My father called.
> His uncle died.
> Your grandfather is ill.

9-29. Sentences. Capitalize the first word of every sentence.

> Run to the end of the street.
> Will he go to the picnic?
> That is the answer!

9-30. Statement Following a Colon. An expression following a colon begins with a capital only if it is a complete sentence.

> He stated his reason: the lateness of the hour.
> He stated his reason: The hour was late.

If a complete sentence or passage follows a colon, the first word of that sentence may or may not begin with a capital letter. The use of a capital gives emphasis to the independent status of the sentence following the colon.

> Aristotle groups occupations according to physical efforts: True arts require the smallest occasions for chance; the most servile jobs call for the greatest physical exertions; and those classed as vulgar have the least need of excellence.

> **Note 1:** If the sentence or sentences following the colon are considered to be a continuation of the introductory sentence, no capital is needed.

> There were two reasons for his action: his work schedule was heavy, and his time was limited.

> **Note 2:** If the sentence following the colon is a quotation, it must begin with a capital letter.

> He stated his reason: "The project is too difficult for the boy."

> **Note 3:** If a list of items follows a colon in a sentence, no capitalization is needed. However, if the items are shown in a tabulation, the first word of each item should be capitalized.

> He ordered the following supplies: stationery, envelopes, carbon paper, pencils, staples, paper clips, erasers, and pens.

> He ordered the following supplies:
> Stationery
> Envelopes
> Carbon paper
> Pencils
> Staples
> Paper clips
> Erasers
> Pens

9-31. Time Periods. Capitalize the names of days of the week, months of the year, holidays, and specially designated days and weeks.

Monday	December
Easter	Fourth of July
Flower Day	Labor Day
Crime Prevention Week	Sweetest Day

Note: Do not capitalize the seasons of the year unless they are personified.

I cannot wait until spring arrives.
I shall take a vacation this summer.
Autumn, sweet Autumn, breathes . . . .

9-32. United States Armed Services. Capitalize the names of the United States Army, Navy, Marines, Air Force, Coast Guard, and their branches.

United States Army	United States Marines
National Guard	Coast Guard Reserves

9-33. Caution About Capitalizing. Do not capitalize some words derived from proper names that have developed a special meaning. In those uses, the words are written with small letters.

bohemian	boycott
italicize	anglicize
china	macadamize
pasteurize	plaster of paris

9-34. Special Styles

Current conventions allow a great deal of latitude in capitalization to achieve special emphasis, a distinctive style, or a special purpose.

In referring to an occasion of special importance, the writer may use capitalization to convey that sense of importance to the reader. An anniversary sale seems more of an important event and more of an institution when written Anniversary Sale or even ANNIVERSARY SALE. A committee on ethical practices gains stature when it is referred to the Committee on Ethical Practices.

A company name may be made more distinctive by capitalizing (or not capitalizing) in a distinctive style. Accuramatic Electronics, Inc. may be written as ACCURAMATIC for brevity and distinction. It might also be written ACCURAMATIC ELECTRONICS, INC.— or even more distinctively, accuramatic electronics, inc.

For general use, each firm should establish standard rules for capitalizing the firm name, the abbreviated firm name if one is used, and the names of the departments and products of the firm.

Even after such a policy is established, special occasions or special documents may require special policies. Minutes or proceedings of the board of directors or the board of trustees may follow the custom used in law: no capitalization unless absolutely necessary. In documents of this kind, the names of committees, offices, departments, products, etc., that might ordinarily be capitalized are used so frequently that the emphasis normally gained by capitalization is lost; and the result is both confusing and unattractive.

Generally accepted conventions should be followed consistently unless some special effect is desired. Even when unusual capitalization is employed for special effect, an appropriate style should be chosen for the occasion; and that style should be used consistently throughout the document.

Unit 10

Spelling Aids

English differs from many other languages in that the spelling of words does not always conform to the sound of the words. The only safe and trustworthy way to learn to spell is by a direct study of words and by acquiring the dictionary habit.

10-1. Words That Are Frequently Misspelled

absence
accelerate
accelerated
accessible
accessory
accidentally
accommodate
accrued
accumulate
achievement
adjacent
advertise
advisable
advisory
affidavit
affiliate
airmail
airport
airtight
alignment
all right
alleged
allergy
alphabetize
analysis
analyze
anchor
annulment
anonymous
apiece
apologize
apostrophe
appraisal
archives
arrears
article
ascertain
assessed
assessment
assignment
assistance
attorneys (*pl.*)
auxiliary

bankruptcy
beginning
believing
beneficiary
benefited
(*or* benefitted)
blueprint
bookkeeper
bookkeeping
bouquet
brochure
bureau
business
businesslike
businessman
businesswoman

cable
campaign
canceling
(*or* cancelling)
cancellation
cannot
casualty
cellophane
changeable
chauffeur
checkoff (*n.*)
checkup (*n.*)
chosen
clientele
collateral
committed
committee
comparable
comparative
comparison
compromise
concede
conference
conferred
congratulate
connoisseur

10

control
controlling
controversy
cooperate
courtesy
courthouse
criticize
crystallize
cynical

debtor
deceive
decision
defense
defensible
deferred
definite
delegate
dependent
desirable
develop
dilemma
diligence
disastrous
dividend

ecstasy
effervescence
efficiency
eliminated
elsewhere
embarrass
embarrassing
emergency
en route
endeavor
enforceable
ensemble
everyday (*adj., n.*)
exaggerate
exasperated
exceed
excel
excise
excitable
excusable
exercise
exhaustion
exhibit
exhilarate
exigency
exorbitant
expedite
extemporaneous
extension
extraordinary

facilitate
fascinating
fifth

fireproof
first-class (*adj., adv.*)
firsthand (*adj., adv.*)
forbearance
foreclosure
foreword
forfeit
forty
fourteen
fraternize
fulfill

gluing
government
governor
grateful
gratis
guaranteeing

handkerchief
harass
height
hindrance
hypothecate

identical
inadvertently
inasmuch as
indestructible
indictment
indispensable
installment
intact
intelligence
intercede
interference'
investigated
irrelevant
issuing
itinerary

judgment
justifiable

label
lacquer
layout
left-hand (*adj.*)
letterhead
liaison
license
lien
liquefy
liquid
litigation
losing
lying

mailbox
maintenance

maneuver
(or manoeuvre
  or manoeuver)
manila
marred
may be (v.)
maybe (adv.)
meantime
mediocre
memorize
merchandise
mileage
miscellaneous
monopolize
mortgage

necessary
negotiate
nephew
nickel
ninety
ninth
nominal
nonresident
noticeable
notifying

obstacle
occasion
occurred
occurrence
occurring
offense
offering
omission
omitted
optimistic
organize
overall (adj., n.)
overcharge
overcome
overhead
oversight

pamphlet
parallel
paralyze
parcel post
pastime
payroll
penetrate
percent
perforated
personnel
persuasion
phenomenal
physician
pickup (n.)
plumber
policyholder

possession
postmortem (adj., n.)
post office (n.)
post-office (adj.)
postal card
postgraduate
precede
preferable
prejudice
preponderance
price list
privacy
privilege
procedure
proceed
professor
profited
promissory
psychology

questionnaire

readjust
recede
receipt
receive
recognize
recommend
referee
referring
regretful
regrettable
remembrance
repetition
restaurant
rewrite
righteous

safety
scarcely
scissors
secondhand (adj., adv.)
semiannual
separate
sergeant
serviceable
set up (v.)
setup (n.)
similar
simultaneous
so-called (adj.)
someday (adv.)
sometime (adj., adv.)
spontaneous
statistician
stimulus
stockroom
subsidiary
subsidize
substantial

subtle
succeed
supersede
supervise
surmise
surprise
susceptible
synonym

tariff
thoroughly
timekeeper
timetable
today
tomorrow
tonight
tranquil
transient
traveler

unanimous
unforgettable

usable
(*or* useable)
utilize

vacillate
vacuum
vice versa
viewpoint

warehouse
weekend (*n., adj., v.*)
welfare
whereas
wholehearted
withhold
worthwhile (*adj.*)
worthwhile (*predicatively*)
write up (*v.*)
write-up (*n.*)

yearbook

10-2. Words That Are Similar in Sound but Different in Meaning

Note: The parenthetical explanations in the following list are merely suggestions to help clarify the meanings. Consult a good dictionary to determine finer distinctions.

accede	(agree)	affect—*v.*	(act upon)
exceed	(surpass)	effect—*v.*	(bring about)
		effect—*n.*	(result)
accent	(stress)		
ascend	(climb)	aid	(assist)
ascent	(motion upward)	aide	(assistant)
assent	(agree)		
		aisle	(passageway)
accept	(receive)	isle	(island)
except	(exclude)		
		allowed	(permitted)
access	(admittance)	aloud	(audibly)
assess	(levy)		
excess	(surplus)	all ready	(prepared)
		already	(by this time)
ad	(advertisement)		
add	(total)	altar	(religious table)
		alter	(change)
adapt	(conform)		
adept	(skillful)	anecdote	(story)
adopt	(take)	antidote	(remedy)
addition	(increase)	any one	(single)
edition	(publication)	anyone	(collectively)
adverse	(contrary)	appraise	(evaluate)
averse	(unwilling)	apprise	(inform)
advice—*n.*	(counsel)	are	(form of *be*)
advise—*v.*	(give counsel)	hour	(time)
		our	(pronoun)
		arraign	(accuse)
		arrange	(organize)

attendance	(presence)
attendants	(escorts)
aught	(at all)
ought	(should)
bail	(security)
bale	(bundle)
bare	(uncovered)
bear	(carry, animal)
bases—*pl.*	(foundations)
basis—*sing.*	(foundation)
bazaar	(market)
bizarre	(fantastic)
berth	(bed)
birth	(origin)
biannual	(twice a year)
biennial	(every two years)
bloc	(group)
block	(piece of wood, etc.)
born	(given birth)
borne	(carried)
bouillon	(broth)
bullion	(gold or silver)
brake	(device)
break	(divide)
breach	(violation)
breech	(lower part)
breadth	(width)
breath	(respiration)
burned	(past of *burn*)
burnt	(p.p. of *burn*)
buy	(purchase)
by	(preposition)
calendar	(almanac)
calender	(roller)
colander	(strainer)
cannon	(mounted gun)
canon	(law or rule)
canyon	(ravine)
canvas	(cloth)
canvass	(solicit)
capital	(principal)
capitol	(building)
carat	(weight)
caret	(the symbol ∧)
carrot	(vegetable)
carton	(box)
cartoon	(caricature)
ceiling	(top)
sealing	(closing)

censer	(vessel)
censor	(critic)
censure	(blame)
cent	(one penny)
scent	(odor)
sent	(past of *send*)
choir	(singers)
quire	(24 sheets)
cite	(quote)
sight	(vision)
site	(location)
close	(finish)
clothes	(garments)
coarse	(rough)
course	(plan)
collision	(clash)
collusion	(fraud)
colonel	(officer)
kernel	(seed)
command	(control)
commend	(praise)
complement	(complete)
compliment	(praise)
confidant—*masc.*	(friend)
confidante—*fem.*	(friend)
confident	(hopeful)
confidence	(certainty)
consul	(foreign representative)
council	(assembly)
counsel	(advice)
core	(center)
corps	(army)
correspondence	(written communication)
correspondent	(one who writes)
corespondent	(one named jointly)
costume	(dress)
custom	(habit)
creak	(noise)
creek	(stream)
credible	(believable)
creditable	(estimable)
currant	(fruit)
current	(up to date)
cymbal	(musical instrument)
symbol	(sign)
decease	(die)
disease	(illness)
decent	(upright)
descend	(move downward)
descent	(ancestry)
dissent	(disagree)

deference	(respect)
difference	(variation)
deferential	(respectful)
differential	(varying)
desert—*n.*	(barren place)
desert—*v.*	(abandon)
dessert	(sweetmeat)
device—*n.*	(contrivance)
devise—*v.*	(scheme)
dice—*n.*	(pl. of die)
dies—*n.*	(pl. of die)
dyes	(colors)
disburse	(pay out)
disperse	(scatter)
divers	(sundry)
diverse	(unlike)
dual	(double)
duel	(combat)
dyeing	(coloring)
dying	(expiring)
elicit	(call forth)
illicit	(unlawful)
eligible	(can be chosen)
illegible	(undecipherable)
elusive	(baffling)
illusive	(deceptive)
emerge	(rise out)
immerge	(plunge)
emigrate	(leave country)
immigrate	(enter country)
eminent	(prominent)
imminent	(threatening)
ere	(before)
e'er	(ever)
err	(mistake)
eruption	(outburst)
irruption	(inburst)
extant	(existent)
extent	(range)
faint	(collapse)
feint	(pretend)
fair	(pleasing)
fare	(fee)
farther	(distance)
further	(advance)
faze	(disconcert)
phase	(aspect)
feat	(act of skill)
feet	(pl. of *foot*)

finally	(lastly)
finely	(excellently)
fiscal	(financial)
physical	(material)
formally	(ceremoniously)
formerly	(before)
forth	(forward)
fourth	(after third)
foul	(unfair)
fowl	(bird)
freeze	(congeal)
frieze	(border)
gamble	(speculate)
gambol	(play)
gap	(opening)
gape	(stare)
gilt	(goldlike)
guilt	(wickedness)
gist	(pith)
jest	(joke)
grate	(frame)
great	(large)
grill	(broil)
grille	(metal fence)
guarantee	(pledge)
guaranty	(contract)
guessed	(conjectured)
guest	(visitor)
handsome	(beautiful)
hansom	(carriage)
heal	(cure)
heel	(part of foot)
hear	(listen)
here	(this place)
hearsay	(rumor)
heresy	(opposing opinion)
hew	(cut)
hue	(color)
higher	(above)
hire	(employ)
hoard	(amass)
horde	(tribe)
hole	(opening)
whole	(entire)
holy	(sacred)
wholly	(entirely)
inapt	(not suitable)
inept	(absurd)

incidence	(range of occurrence)	marshal	(officer)
incidents	(events)	martial	(warlike)
		marital	(marriage)
incite	(arouse)		
insight	(understanding)	material	(goods)
		materiel	(equipment)
indict	(accuse)		
indite	(compose)	mean	(average)
		mien	(manner)
ingenious	(clever)		
ingenuous	(frank)	medal	(reward)
		meddle	(interfere)
instance	(occasion)		
instants	(moments)	metal	(ore)
		mettle	(courage)
interstate	(between states)		
intrastate	(within one state)	miner	(worker)
		minor	(under age)
its	(possessive pronoun)		
it's	(it is)	monetary	(financial)
		monitory	(warning)
knew	(past of *know*)		
new	(not old)	moral	(ethical)
		morale	(spirit)
know	(perceive directly)		
no	(negative)	morning	(part of day)
		mourning	(grief)
lead	(metal)		
led	(past of *lead*)	motif	(theme)
		motive	(reason)
lean	(thin, rely)		
lien	(legal claim)	ordinance	(decree)
		ordnance	(artillery)
leased	(rented)		
least	(smallest)	overdo	(overwork)
		overdue	(tardy)
lessen	(diminish)		
lesson	(instruction)	pain	(hurt)
		pane	(window)
lesser	(inferior)		
lessor	(landlord)	pair	(two of a kind)
		pare—*v.*	(peel)
liable	(accountable)	pear	(fruit)
libel	(written slander)		
		passed	(past of *pass*)
lightening	(unburdening)	past	(gone by)
lighting	(illuminating)		
lightning	(discharge of atmospheric electricity)	patience	(composure)
		patients	(people under medical care)
load	(quantity)		
lode	(mineral deposit)	peace	(calm)
		piece	(part)
loan	(something lent)		
lone	(one)	pedal	(treadle)
		peddle	(offer for sale from place to place)
loath	(unwilling)		
loathe	(detest)	persecuted	(ill-treated)
		prosecuted	(sued)
local	(sectional)		
locale	(locality)	personal	(private)
		personnel	(staff)
loose—*adj.*	(unbound)		
lose—*v.*	(miss)	perspective	(mental aspect)
		prospective	(expected)
magnate	(person of rank)		
magnet	(lodestone)	plain	(unadorned)
		plane	(level)
manner	(mode)		
manor	(mansion)		

plaintiff	(accuser)	sleight	(artful)
plaintive	(mournful)	slight	(trivial)
practicable	(feasible)	stationary	(stable)
practical	(useful)	stationery	(paper)
precede	(go before)	statue	(image)
proceed	(go ahead)	statute	(law)
precedence	(rank)	stile	(barrier)
precedent	(standard)	style	(fashion)
president	(head)		
		straight	(unbroken)
presence	(attendance)	strait	(narrow pass)
presents	(gifts)		
		suit	(legal application)
principal	(chief, capital)	suite	(matched group)
principle	(rule)	sweet	(opposite of sour)
profit	(gain)	superintendence	(management)
prophet	(seer)	superintendents	(supervisors)
prophecy	(prediction)	tail	(appendage)
prophesy	(foretell)	tale	(story)
propose	(suggest)	tare	(allowance)
purpose	(intention)	tear	(to rip)
raise	(lift)	than	(in comparison)
rays	(beams)	then	(at that time)
raze	(destroy)		
		their	(belonging to them)
rap	(knock)	there	(in that place)
wrap	(enclose)	they're	(they are)
reality	(truth)	therefor	(for it)
realty	(real estate)	therefore	(consequently)
reign	(rule)	threw	(past of *throw*)
rein	(halter)	through	(by means of)
residence	(home)	tier	(row or layer)
residents	(persons)	tear	(drop of fluid)
right	(correct)	to	(preposition)
rite	(ceremony)	too	(also)
wright	(worker)	two	(one plus one)
write	(express)		
		topography	(geographical)
role	(a part)	typography	(from type)
roll	(a list)		
		track	(footprint)
roomer	(lodger)	tract	(treatise)
rumor	(hearsay)		
		waist	(bodice)
root	(part of a plant)	waste	(refuse)
route	(a course or path)		
		waive	(set aside)
seize	(grasp)	wave	(signal)
siege	(battle)		
		ware	(goods)
serial	(sequential)	wear	(clothe)
cereal	(food)	where	(whither)
session	(conference)	weak	(feeble)
cession	(yielding)	week	(seven days)
shear	(cut)	weather	(temperature)
sheer	(thin)	whether	(if)
sight	(vision)	who's	(who is)
site	(place, position)	whose	(possessive)

10-3. Memory Aids to Overcome Troublesome Words

For troublesome words that occur again and again, an individual may establish his own memory aids or mnemonic devices to help him overcome the tendency to misspell.

1. Prefix

> *h* to *ear* (organ of hearing) and you have *hear*, meaning to perceive with the ear.
> *t* to *here* (in this place) and you have *there*, meaning in that place.
> *t* to *heir* (one who inherits) and you have *their*, meaning belonging to them.

2. Associate

> *e* in *stationery* with the *e* in *letter*, since it is chiefly used for letter writing.
> *a* in *stationary* with the *a* in *stable*, for their meanings are synonymous.
> *a* in *affect* (verb only) and the *e* in *effect* (verb and noun) with their respective definitions: affect, to *act* upon; effect (noun), result; and effect (verb), to accomplish a result.

3. Acronyms

> Devise words formed from the first letter of each of several related words. For example, GEOGRAPHY: George eats our great rice and paints houses yellow.

10-4. Commonly Used Foreign Expressions and Words

KEY			
Ar.	Arabic	It.	Italian
F.	French	J.	Japanese
G.	German	L.	Latin
Gr.	Greek	Sc.	Scandinavian
H.	Hawaiian	Sp.	Spanish

adiós	(Sp., ăd'ĭ·ōs')	farewell
agenda	(L., á·jĕn'dá)	list of things to be done
à la mode	(F., ä'lá·mōd'; ăl'á·mōd'; ä lä mōd')	served with ice cream
alma mater	(L., ăl'má mä'tēr; ăl'má mä'tēr)	one's college, university, or school
aloha	(H., ä·lō'hä)	greeting or farewell
auf Wiedersehen	(G., ouf' vē'dēr·zā'ĕn; -zän')	till we meet again
au gratin	(F., ō' grá'tăN'; Angl. ō, or ô, grät''n)	served with cheese or browned crumbs
au revoir	(F., ō' rē·vwár')	till we meet again
bona fide	(L., bō'ná fī'dê)	genuine; in good faith
bon jour	(F., bôN' zhōōr')	good day; good morning
bon soir	(F., bôN' swär')	good evening
bon vivant	(F., bôN' vē'väN')	person with cultivated or refined tastes
bon voyage	(F., bôN' vwá'yàzh')	a farewell phrase
bravo	(It., brä'vō; brā'vō)	shout of applause
brochure	(F., brô·shōōr'; shür')	a pamphlet

café	(F., kå'fä')	coffeehouse; restaurant
carte blanche	(F., kärt' bláNsh'; *F.* kårt')	full discretionary power
caveat emptor	(L., kā'vẻ·ăt ĕmp'tôr)	let the buyer beware (**Law**)
chaise longue	(F., shāz' lôNg'; *F.* shâz')	long chair for half-sitting, half-reclining position
chic	(F., shēk; shĭk)	cleverly stylish
coiffure	(F., kwä·fūr')	hairdo
communiqué	(F., kŏ·mū'nĭ·kā' *or, esp. Brit.,* kŏ·mū'nĭ·kā)	information given officially
connoisseur	(F., kŏn'ĭ·sûr'; sūr')	a critical expert
cortege	(F., kôr·tĕzh'; -tāzh'. Also cor'tège) kôr'tĕzh')	a retinue
coup d'etat	(F., kōō dā'tà')	an unexpected stroke of policy
cuisine	(F., kwẻ·zēn')	manner or style of cooking; the kitchen
cum laude	(L., kŭm lô'dē; kŏŏm lou'dĕ)	with highest honors
danseuse	(F., däN'sûz')	woman ballet dancer
data	(L., dā'tà; dä'tà)	facts
debonair	(F., dĕb'ȯ·nâr')	light-hearted; courteous; gracious
debut	(F., dā'bū; då·bū')	first apearance before the public
encore	(F., äng'kŏr)	further performance; again
entree	(F., än'trā; *F.* äN'trā')	a dish served as the chief course
e pluribus unum	(L., ē plōō'rĭ·bŭs ū'nŭm; plōŏr'ĭ·bŭs)	one out of many
esprit de corps	(F., ĕs'prē'; ĕs'prē dē kôr')	common spirit pervading members of a group
ex officio	(L., ĕks ȯ·fĭsh'ĭ·ō)	by virtue of an office
facade	(F., fà·säd'; fä-)	front of a building
faux pas	(F., fō' pä')	false step; mistake
foyer	(F., foi'ā; foi'ēr; fwä'yā)	lobby
gemuetlichkeit	(G., gĕ müt lĭk kīt')	geniality
gourmet	(F., gōōr'mā; *F.* gōōr'mĕ')	an epicure; a connoisseur in eating or drinking
habeas corpus	(L., hā'bẻ·ăs kôr'pŭs)	a writ requiring a person to be brought into court
hara-kiri	(J., hăr'à·kĭr'ĭ; hä'rà-)	Japanese suicide
hors d'oeuvre	(F., dů'vr' ; *pl.* D'OEUVRES dů'vr)	relish or appetizer
ibid. (ibidem)	(L., ĭ·bī'dĕm)	in the same place
in absentia	(L., ĭn ăb·sĕn'shĭ·à)	in absence
kudos	(Gr., kū'dŏs; kōō'dŏs)	renown, praise
laissez faire	(F., lĕ'sā' fâr')	noninterference; unconcern
lei	(H., lā'ẻ; lā)	wreath or garland of leaves or flowers
maître d'hôtel	(F., mâ'trē dô'tĕl'; mât' dô'tĕl')	chief employee in a hotel or restaurant
mousse	(F., mōōs)	frozen dessert made with whipped cream
nee	(F., nā)	born; refers to the maiden name
nom de plume	(F., nŏm' dē plōōm')	pen name
per annum	(L., pẽr ăn'ŭm)	by the year
per capita	(L., pẽr kăp'ĭ·tà)	by the head
per diem	(L., pẽr dī'ĕm)	by the day
per se	(L., pûr sē)	itself
posse	(L., pŏs'ẻ)	crowd with legal authority
pro rata	(L., prō rā'tà; rä'tà)	in proportion to
prosit	(G., prō'sĭt)	a drinking toast
protégé	(F., prō'tĕ·zhā)	one under special care of another
proximo	(L., prŏk'sĭ·mō)	nearest; in the next month after the present one
re	(L., rē)	in or of the thing; matter of
rendezvous	(F., rän'dĕ·vōō; rĕn'-)	secret meeting place; meeting by appointment

repertoire	(F., rĕp′ēr·twär; -twôr)	collection of rehearsed selections
répondez s'il vous plaît	(F., râ′ pôn′ dā′ sēl vōō plĕ′)	answer, if you please (abbr. R.S.V.P.)
résumé	(F., rā′zû·mā′; F. rā′zü′mā′)	summary
safari	(Ar., sȧ·fä′rĭ)	expedition
sans	(F., sănz; F. säN)	without
semper fidelis	(L., sĕm′pēr fĭ·dē′lĭs)	always faithful
sine die	(L., sī′nė dī′ē)	without apointing a day
skoal	(Sc., skōl)	a drinking toast
status quo	(L., stā′tŭs; stăt′ŭs kwō)	current state
sub rosa	(F., sŭb rō′zȧ)	furtive; secret
table d'hôte	(F., tȧ′blē dōt′; tä′b'l)	a meal for which one pays a fixed price
tempus fugit	(L., tĕm′pŭs fū′jĭt)	time flies
tête à tête	(F., tät′ ȧ tät′; tĕ′-tȧ tât′)	intimate conversation between two persons
touché	(F., tōō′shā′)	to acknowledge a successful point
ultimo	(L., ŭl′tĭ·mō)	in the month preceding the present
versus	(L., vûr′sŭs)	against
vice versa	(L., vĭ′sė vû′sȧ)	the reverse
vox populi	(L., vŏks pŏp′ů·lĭ)	voice of the people

10-5. A Guide to Pronunciation

Nations are no longer isolated from each other. The vast interchange of correspondence today is making it necessary for lexicographers to include the diacritical marks of both the American System (Am.) and the International Phonetic Association (IPA). The parallel markings and illustrative words from the two systems follow.

VOWELS AND DIPTHONGS

Am.	IPA	Illustrations	Am.	IPA	Illustrations
ā	eɪ	cake, pay	ō	o	hoe, so
a̱	e	chaotic	ŏ	ɒ	lock
ă	æ	mat	ô	ɔ	off, loss
ä	ɑ	father, hearth	ū, ōō	u	use, pool
â	ɛə	care, there	ŭ, ŏŏ	ʊ	pull, look
ē	i	see	ŭ	ʌ	pump
ĕ	ɛ	edge	au	ɔ	caught
ē, û	ɝ	marker, turn	oi, oy	ɔɪ	coil, toy
ī, ȳ	aɪ	ice, aisle, fly	ou	aʊ	thou, foul
ĭ, ў	ɪ	if, tymbal			

CONSONANTS

Am.	IPA	Illustrations
b	b	bib
ç	s	cease
¢	k	cook
ch	tʃ	choke
¢h	k	chorus
çh	ʃ	chaise
d	˙d	did
f	f	file
ġ	ʒ	gem
g	g	get, goal
h	h	him
j	dʒ	jell, just
k	k	keen, kill
l	l	lull
m	m	may, mill
n	n	now, nail
ng	ŋ	sing
p	p	pod, pan
q	kw	quail, quit

CONSONANTS (Concluded)

Am.	IPA	Illustrations
r	r	red, rare
s	s	sold, sum
sh	ʃ	mesh
t	t	tot
th	θ	thin, thigh
th	ð	then
v	v	valley, vile
w	w	was, wiles
wh	hw	what, why
x, ks	ks	exit
x, gz	gz	exist
y	j	yet
z	z	zeal
zh, s, g	ʒ	azure, measure garage

NON-ENGLISH VOWELS AND CONSONANTS

Am.	IPA	Illustrations
il	i:j	Fr., fille
eu	ø	Fr., deux
ö	ø	Gr., schön
ö	œ	Gr., können
u	y	Fr., rue
ü	y	Gr., grün
ch, ᴋ	ç	Gr., ich; Scot., heich
ch, ᴋ˙	x	Gr., ach; Scot., loch

Hyphenation

Hyphenation is complex. An unabridged dictionary should be the final authority whenever problems arise. Convention is changing; more and more, hyphens are used only when it is necessary to clarify or to emphasize.

11-1. When to Use a Hyphen

1. **Compound Numbers.** Compound numbers from twenty-one through ninety-nine are hyphened.

sixty-nine	twenty-eight million
one hundred and thirty-five	two hundred (no hyphen)
forty-seven hundred	seventeen (no hyphen)

2. **Compound Adjectives with Numerals.** When numerals are used before other words to form compound adjectives, a hyphen is used.

   28-story building
   eight- *or* 8-cylinder motor
   four-year-old child
   15-day trial period (15 days' trial)
   20-minute lecture

3. **Double Compounds.** Double compounds having a common base are hyphened.

   two- and five-pound boxes
   long- and short-term policies

4. **Fractions.** A fraction expressed in words and used as an adjective requires a hyphen between the numerator and the denominator.

   A three-fourths vote is necessary. (¾)
   One-half year's credit will be given. (½)

   Note 1: When a fraction expressed in words is used as a noun, no hyphen is required.

   Three fourths of the votes were cast for the amendment.
   One half of the money must be raised by June.

   Note 2: Care must be used in writing fractions when the denominator is hundredths, thousandths, etc. The hyphen is placed for clarity of meaning.

twenty-one hundredths (21/100)	sixty-nine thousandths (69/1000)
twenty one-hundredths (20/100)	sixty nine-thousandths (60/9000)

11

5. Compounds with Prepositions. Compound adjectives and many nouns having a preposition as the second member should be hyphened.

ADJECTIVE	NOUN
well-to-do merchant	lean-to
follow-up letter	tie-up
worn-out tires	tie-in
built-in cupboard	hanger-on

6. Compound Adjectives Before Nouns. Two or more words used as a single modifier and preceding a noun should be hyphened.

well-known writer	better-than-average typist
middle-aged woman	self-made man
first-class mail	fire-resistant building
hard-of-hearing student	no-par-value stock

Note 1: The purpose of hyphenation in the following examples is to tie together the adjectives that express a single modifying idea. See also the note under Rule 8-17:6 on page 62.

an intelligent well-known writer
a handsome middle-aged man

Note 2: When one of the words in a compound modifier ends in the comparative or superlative *er* or *est*, no hyphen is needed.

high-pitched	low-pressure
higher pitched	lower pressure

Note 3: When an expression that would ordinarily be hyphened *follows* the noun, no hyphens are necessary.

The writer is well known.   The project was ill planned.

7. For Convenience. Some words are hyphened to avoid tripling of consonants.

bell-like   shell-less

8. Improvised Words. Improvised or conventionalized words require hyphens.

lemon-yellow (adj.)	L-shaped
blue-pencil (v.)	U-curve
jack-o'-lantern	single-space (v.)
helter-skelter	happy-go-lucky
X-ray (adj., v.) *but* X ray (noun)	

9. For Clarity. Words whose meanings may be misinterpreted or ambiguous should be hyphened.

re-cite (cite again)	recite (narrate)
re-cover (cover again)	recover (repossess)
re-create (create again)	recreate (amuse)
re-treat (treat again)	retreat (withdraw)

11

10. Compounds with Possessives. Some compounds that have a possessive noun as the first member are hyphened. It is best to consult a dictionary for such words.

    crow's-feet   cat's-paw

11. Words with Prefixes. Most *self, ex,* and *vice* words are hyphened. The hyphen is used also to join a prefix to a proper name.

    self-control   ex-secretary
    self-defense   un-American
    vice-president   pro-French

    Exceptions: selfish   selfsame   oneself

12. The hyphen is also a punctuation mark. See Unit 8, page 71.

11-2. When Not to Use a Hyphen

1. Titles. Most civil and military titles and designations of official positions are not hyphened.

    Secretary of State
    editor in chief
    major general
    purchasing agent
    general manager

2. Ordinary Compounds. Combinations of ordinary words used in regular order and as modifiers are generally not hyphened.

    civil service work   real estate tax
    social service secretary   high school teacher
    motion picture films   safe deposit box
    income tax form   fire insurance company
    long distance call   elementary school text

3. Suffix "ly." A combination of an adverb ending in *ly* and an adjective is not hyphened.

    carefully laid plans
    eagerly anxious mother
    slowly moving trains
    hastily written letter

    Note: Do not confuse adjectives ending in *ly* with adverbs.

    a manly decision   curly hair

4. Proper Names and Adjectives. Proper names composed of two words used as adjectives are not hyphened, but adjectives compounded from two proper names require hyphens.

    New England states   Anglo-Saxon records
    North American Indian   Washington-Pittsburgh
                                 route

5. Compounds with Prefixes. Most words compounded with the following prefixes are written solid: *bi, circum, fore, inter, mis, mono, over, super, tri, under, up, where.*

biannual	overburden
circumscribe	supersede
forefather	tricycle
interoffice	underbrush
misplace	upstage
monosyllable	wherein

6. Proper Names with Prefixes. The prefixes *ante, anti, hyper, non, post, pre, pro, semi, trans,* and *un,* when combined with common words, are usually written solid; when combined with proper names, they are hyphened.

antedate	ante-Victorian
antituberculin	anti-Bohemian
hypertension	hyper-Lydian
noncoherent	non-Shakespearean
postmaster	post-Homeric
precaution	pre-Columbian
proportion	pro-English
semiannual	semi-Norman
transcontinental	trans-African
unbecoming	un-American

Word Division

In all types of correspondence, the end-of-line division of words should be reduced to a minimum. When separation of a word is necessary, the division should be based on the principles of pronunciation, spelling, and balance. Balance in this instance refers to retaining a readable portion of the word on the first line. The division of a word as shown in an unabridged dictionary should be qualified by the application of the following principles and guides.

Note: In these illustrations both the diagonal and the dot show word division. The diagonal is used to show recommended points at which words may be divided at the ends of lines; the dot is used to show acceptable, but not preferred, division points.

12-1. The most desirable point at which to divide a word is sometimes a matter of opinion. However, it is preferable to have enough of the word on the first line to suggest the entire word and to carry to the next line enough of the word to have two significantly sized parts. Pronunciation of the word is also an important factor in the determination of the best division point.

sug·ges/tion	ad·min/is/tra/tion
rep·re/sent	may·on/naise

12-2. Divide words only between syllables. One-syllable words must not be divided.

lei/sure	length/wise
con·sti/tute	mea/sure
far/ther	fol/lowed
called	rolled
drowned	strength
through	freight
edge	shipped

12-3. There must be more than one letter with the first part of the word and more than two letters with the last part of the word.

around	*not*	a-round
elapsed	*not*	e-lapsed
lately	*not*	late-ly
marker	*not*	mark-er
teacher	*not*	teach-er
friendly	*not*	friend-ly
press/ing		teach/ing
con/form		re·lated
ad·heres		fric/tion

Note: Setting off a two-letter syllable at the beginning of a word is acceptable, but such a division is not recommended.

113

12-4. Do not divide a word of five or fewer letters, even though it may have two syllables. If possible, avoid dividing a word of six letters.

about	*not*	a-bout
badly	*not*	bad-ly
today	*not*	to-day
topic	*not*	top-ic
sudden	*rather than*	sud·den
devise	*rather than*	de·vise
advice	*rather than*	ad·vice
letter	*rather than*	let·ter
deduct	*rather than*	de·duct
cattle	*rather than*	cat·tle

12-5. When a final consonant, preceded by a single vowel, is doubled before a suffix is added, divide between the two consonants.

get/ting	com/pel/ling
re·fer/ring	jog/ging
flip/ping	per/mit/ting
skim/ming	slip/ping

12-6. When a root word ends in a double consonant before a suffix is added, divide between the root word and the suffix.

will/ing	re·press/ing
spell/ing	as·sess/ing

12-7. When dividing words ending in *cial, tial, cion, sion, tion, sive,* and *tive,* keep the endings as separate units.

di·rec/tion	dis·cus/sion
re·flec/tion	in·den/tion
im·par/tial	in·struc/tive
bene·fi/cial	re·gres/sive

12-8. If a compound word is written with a hyphen, divide the compound only at the point of the existing hyphen.

old-/fashioned   self-/employed

12-9. If a compound word is written without a hyphen, divide between the elements of the compound.

busi·ness/men	man/ser·vant
let·ter/head	nev·er/the/less

12

12-10. If a single-letter syllable falls within a word, write the syllable with the first part of the word.

regu/late   tabu/late
gaso/line   crea/tion
speci/fied   ma·nipu/late

Note 1: An exception to this rule occurs when a single-vowel syllable immediately precedes an ending two-letter syllable. Both syllables should be carried over to the next line.

read/ily   stead/ily

Note 2: A second exception to this rule occurs when the single-letter syllable *a, i,* or *u* is followed by the ending syllable *ble, bly, cle,* or *cal.* Both syllables should be carried over to the next line.

laud/able   cler/ical
mir/acle   fa·vor/ably

12-11. If 2 one-letter syllables occur together within a word, divide between the one-letter syllables.

gradu/ation   con·tinu/ation
anxi/ety   evacu/ation

12-12. If it is necessary to divide parts of a date, a proper name, or an address, divide at the logical point for readbility.

April 12,/19--   (between the day and the year)
Mr. John/Smith   (not between *Mr.* and the name)
Roy R./Ames, M.D.   (not between the name and the degree)
Chicago,/Illinois 60616 (between the city and state names)

12-13. If possible, avoid dividing figures, abbreviations, and signs representing words or abbreviations.

$15,000   *not* $15, on Line 1 and 000 on Line 2
P & G   *not*   P on Line 1 and & G on Line 2
#231   *not*   # on Line 1 and 231 on Line 2

12-14. Do not separate contractions.

couldn't   isn't   they're   you'll

12-15. Avoid dividing the last word of more than two consecutive lines.

12-16. Avoid dividing the last word of a paragraph or the last word on a page.

12-17. When you decide the point at which to end a line, you should remember that how the line ends determines to a considerable degree the ease with which the reader can follow the thought of the sentence. For this reason, the division of words should be kept to a minimum; and, when such division is necessary, you should make the break in the word a logical one.

Expression of Numbers

Figures are effective because of their eye appeal, their brevity, and the ease with which they can be read. When a choice between expressing numbers in figures or words is necessary, the convenience of the reader and the nature of the document should be considered.

13-1. General Conventions

1. **Number Ten and Under.** As a general rule, spell out number ten and under, except when used with numbers above ten. Also, spell out indefinite amounts. Numbers above ten are written in figures.

. . . six or seven chairs	90 orders
. . . 15 days	about a thousand dollars
7 desks, 9 chairs, and 11 cabinets	

2. **Numbers in Directions.** For ease of reading and for emphasis, all numbers—regardless of size—may be written as figures in directions.

    > Type the following report with a 2-inch top margin and 1-inch side margins (65 pica spaces, 78 elite spaces).

3. **Number Beginning a Sentence.** Always spell out a number if it begins a sentence. If the number is large and cannot be conveniently expressed in words, rearrange the sentence.

    > Thirty-six applications were received.
    > The attendance at the baseball game was 11,346.

4. **Two Numbers Together.** When two numbers are used together, spell out the shorter number and write the longer one in figures.

    > twelve 25-inch pipes   fifteen 32-page booklets

5. **Series of Numbers.** Use figures to express a series of numbers within the same sentence.

    > Mr. E. J. Walters reported the sale of 48 new cars, 228 used cars, and 17 trucks.

6. **Age.** Express approximate age in words; state exact age in figures.

    > He is twenty-two years old.
    > She is 3 years 2 months 10 days old.

    Note: This general convention may be ignored to achieve special effects—particularly in legal documents and other formal papers.

    > He is twenty-two (22) years old.

7. **Distance.** Use figures for distances unless a fraction of a mile is indicated.

    > 82 miles   one-half mile

8. Numbers with Nouns. Express in figures numbers that follow nouns, as *chapter, volume, page, floor, apartment, room,* etc. In the body of a reference, *page* may be written in lower case.

Refer to Chapter IV, page 61.   Volume XII is on loan.
Look at Apartment 1606.   The meeting is in Room 10.

9. Numbers from 21 to 99. Use hyphens in numbers between 21 and 99 when the numbers are written in words.

three thousand four hundred seventy-eight

10. Numbers with Symbols. Do not space between numbers and symbols associated with them.

#47 $5   37%   6¢   14*

11. Unrelated Numbers. Separate unrelated contiguous numbers with commas.

Although there were 50, 51 had to be accounted for.

13-2. Addresses

1. Numbers as Street Names. Spell out all street numbers from one to ten inclusive; write in figures any street number that is 11 or above.

4830 South Third Street   1349 - 15th Avenue
5962-A North First Street   716 East 49 Place

Note: The use of the suffix (st, d, th) after the street number is optional.

2. House and Building Numbers. Express house numbers and building numbers in figures, except in the case of *ONE.*

9 Ridgeway Park
One Regent Street

3. ZIP Codes. Write a Zip Code without commas and separated from the state name by two spaces.

Cincinnati, Ohio   45220   Cleveland, OH   44116

13-3. Dates and Times of Day

1. Datelines. Use figures in datelines in regular correspondence.

December 15, 19----
15 December 19---- (military)

2. Formal Datelines. Use words for unusual effects or formal datelines.

December   December fifteen, nineteen hundred----
fifteen   *or*
19 - - -   Fifteenth of December
    Nineteen hundred----

3. Short Form of Datelines. Follow the short form for datelines in interoffice mail, tabulated reports, and billing.

2-15-19-- 5/7/19--

4. Dates in Letter Body. In the text of a letter or report, express dates in figures.

The report of January 15, 19--, has been filed.
All invoices dated June 1 should be discounted today.

5. Decades and Centuries. Write decades and centuries either in words or in numbers. The name of a decade or a century may be capitalized or not as the author chooses.

in the nineties	the eighteenth century
in the 90s	the 18th century
in the 1920s	the twentieth century

Note: Some authorities use an apostrophe before the "s" in an expression denoting a decade. This form also is permissible.

in the 90's in the 1920's

6. Time of Day. Express the time of the day in any of the following forms:

The bell will ring at five minutes of nine.
The bell will ring at 8:55 a.m., and at 4:00 p.m.

He made an appointment for
⎧ eight or nine-thirty.
⎨ eight o'clock.
⎩ 8 o'clock.

7. Military Time. Military times of day identify hours from 1 through 24 without the use of A.M. or P.M.

1:05 a.m.	0105
Noon	1200
5:00 p.m.	1700
Midnight	2400

13-4. Fractions and Decimals

1. As Adjectives and Nouns. When fractions are used as adjectives, they are written in words and are hyphened. As isolated nouns, they are written as two words without a hyphen. A series of fractions is expressed in figures.

He received a one-fourth share of the estate.
His share equaled one fourth of the estate.
John, Mary, and Paul received ¼, ¼, and ½ of the estate respectively.

2. Mixed Numbers. Express mixed numbers (whole numbers and fractions) in figures.

128 3/5 114 1/2 1 3/4

3. Decimals. Always write decimals in figures—not in words.

0.45 inch
specific gravity 1.3000

4. Consistency in Use. Within the same document, be consistent.

1/2, 1/4, and 7/8 *not* ½, ¼, and 7/8.

13-5. Money, Interest, and Percent

1. Sums of Money. Express sums of money in figures except in legal documents. (See Rule 13-6.) Write even sums without the decimal point and the ciphers.

$7.33   90 cents *not* .90 $10

2. Interest Periods. Express in figures interest periods that include the year, the month, and the day. Do not use commas in such figures.

interest for 3 years 7 months and 4 days

3. Percentages. Express percentages when used in text as follows:

We will allow 6 percent discount.
. . . discounts of 40, 10, and 5%. *or* . . . 40%, 10%, and 5% discounts.
He purchased a 6% Gold Serial Bond.

13-6. Numbers in Legal Documents

1. Sums of Money. In legal work, express sums of money in words followed by figures in parentheses.

. . . the sum of Five Hundred (500) Dollars.
. . . the sum of Five Hundred Dollars ($500).

2. Dates. In legal work, use the ordinal ending or write the date in full.

WITNESSETH this 10th day of November, 19--.

or

WITNESSETH this tenth day of June, nineteen hundred fifty-nine.
. . . as given on the 3d of May.
. . . as given on the third of May.

13-7. Plurals of Figures and Ordinal Endings

1. Plural Forms. Form the plural of figures (except in stock market quotations or other instances in which the author prefers to omit the apostrophe without sacrificing clarity) by adding *'s*.

7's   32's
There are too many 8's in your answer.
There are too many 8s in your answer.

2. Ordinals. Use the ordinal endings *d, st,* and *th* only when the name of the month is omitted or when the day of the month precedes the name of the month.

. . . as given on the { 3d or third
                       { 21st of May

13-8. Tables and Data Reports

1. Sums of Money. In tabulations, memorandums, interoffice forms, and reports of summarized data, the following styles are permissible:

90¢	$.90	$0.90	$1.00

2. Terms. In tabulations, invoices, memorandums, and interoffice forms, use the appropriate symbol.

50%   net 30, 2% ten days   *or*   n/30, 2/10

3. Stock Items, Serials, Policy Numbers. Figures used to represent items, stock numbers, serials, policy numbers, etc., should be preceded by *No.* when used in the text. The symbol # is used in tabulations and short forms. (The symbol #, when placed before a figure, means *Number*; when placed after a figure, *pounds*.)

. . . cancel policy No. 198734687.
Lot No. 48 will be sold soon.   *or*   Lot #75 (memo form)
Serial No. KHM202745-X has been destroyed.

4. Stock Quotations. Use figures for brokerage descriptions and market quotations.

Southern Pacific 4s are being offered now.
. . . stock listed at 110.4
. . . and accrued interest to yield 98.

5. Measures and Other Numerical Quantities. Use figures for measures, dimensions, temperature readings, election returns, and chemical terms.

36 bushels   48° *or* 48 degrees
6 lb. 4 oz.   947 majority
5 ft. 9 in. H_2O
9' x 12' *or* 9 by 12 feet

13-9. Round Numbers and Large Numbers

1. Spelling of Number Part. To avoid the use of many ciphers, the words "billion," "million," and sometimes "thousand" may be spelled out after a number. Note that "hundred" is not spelled out after a number.

$15 billion   7.3 million   9⅔ millions

Note: Large numbers may be written in figures if special emphasis is desired.

2. Expression of Round Numbers. Express a round number, such as 1,500, in hundreds rather than in thousands.

twelve hundred men
not one thousand two hundred men

Note: In formal legal work, such as the writing of wills, the year is written in words in the following manner: in the year of our Lord one thousand nine hundred and sixty-nine.

3. Separating Numbers into Groups. Numbers that are composed of four or more figures are separated by commas into groups of threes from the right to facilitate reading. Serial numbers, telephone, policy, year, page, and room numbers are not separated.

1,478,900	Form No. 5468745
$357,869,452.38	Policy No. 67530245

13-10. Arabic and Roman Numerals

1. While practically all references to numbers require the use of Arabic symbols, Roman numerals are frequently used to designate volume, chapter, and section headings. Roman numerals are also used for the main headings in outlines.

2. To type numbers in either style, follow the practice of keeping an even right margin. Use the tabulator bar or key to expedite writing columns of figures.

ARABIC FIGURES AND EQUIVALENT ROMAN NUMERALS							
1	I	11	XI	30	XXX	400	CCCC
2	II	12	XII	40	XL	500	D
3	III	13	XIII	50	L	600	DC
4	IV	14	XIV	60	LX	700	DCC
5	V	15	XV	70	LXX	800	DCCC
6	VI	16	XVI	80	LXXX	900	CM
7	VII	17	XVII	90	XC	1,000	M
8	VIII	18	XVIII	100	C	2,000	MM
9	IX	19	XIX	200	CC	5,000	$\overline{\text{V}}$*
10	X	20	XX	300	CCC	10,000	$\overline{\text{X}}$*

3. Other combinations of Roman numerals are built by prefixing or annexing letters. The prefixing of a letter is equivalent to subtracting the value of that letter, while the annexing is equivalent to addition.

49 is L minus X plus IX   *or* XLIX
64 is L plus X plus IV   *or* LXIV

---

* A line over a numeral multiplies the value by 1,000.

Abbreviations and Symbols

As advancing technology increases the complexity of communication, the business community seeks more efficient methods of transmitting ideas. Although the use of many of the old familiar abbreviations in formal business correspondence is still frowned upon, the military use of abbreviations and acronyms has led to an increase in the use of initials and telescoped words in business correspondence.

In the use of abbreviations and acronyms, one should observe the conventions. The names of some organizations are *customarily* abbreviated (NASA, BBC). The use of an abbreviation is frequently a superior method of communication because the meaning of the shortened form is more immediately apparent than is the full wordage (AFL-CIO versus American Federation of Labor and Congress of Industrial Organizations).

Military correspondence sanctions the omission of periods within and after all abbreviations expressed in capital letters. This convention is increasingly applied in nonmilitary writing.

Use abbreviations when they clarify or when they save time without sacrificing clarity of expression or quality of form. Do not use abbreviations when they destroy the tone of formality required of some correspondence; do not use abbreviations when they detract from the impact of the material; do not abbreviate ordinary words in business letters. Never use abbreviations to excess, as in the following example:

> It came to the attn. of his atty. that the bal. of the bbls. were dld. in the a.m.

In making up the lists of abbreviations in this unit, the authors used three reference books as the authorities for capitalization and punctuation of the abbreviations:

> *Style Manual,* Rev. ed. Washington: U.S. Government Printing Office, January, 1967.
> *United States Government Organization MANUAL,* 1969-1970. Washington: U. S. Government Printing Office, 1969.
> *The Random House Dictionary of the English Language.* New York: Random House, Inc., 1967.

It should be noted that there are variations in the use of periods with, and in capitalization of, abbreviations. Therefore, for many of the abbreviations given in this unit, there are other acceptable forms.

14-1. Common Abbreviations

A.A.A.	American Automobile Association, Amateur Athletic Association
A.B.A.	American Bankers Association; American Bar Association

14

ABC, A.B.C.	American Broadcasting Company
a.c.	alternating current
acct.	account
A.D.	in the year of our Lord (*anno Domini*)
ad val.	in proportion to the value (*ad valorem*)
AFL-CIO	American Federation of Labor and Congress of Industrial Organizations
A.L.A.	American Library Association
AM	amplitude modulation (radio)
a.m.	before noon (*ante meridiem*)
A.M.A.	American Medical Association, American Management Association
amt.	amount
anon.	anonymous
ans.	answer
AP	Associated Press
assn.	association
asst.	assistant
Attn., Atten., Att.	Attention
atty.	attorney
Ave.	avenue
a.w.o.l.	absent without official leave
bal.	balance
B.B.C.	British Broadcasting Corporation
bbl.	barrel
B.C.	before Christ
B/E, b.e.	bill of exchange
B/F	brought forward
b/l, b.l.	bill of lading
Bldg.	building
Blvd.	boulevard
b.o.	buyer's option
Bro., Bros.	brother, brothers
B.t.u.	British thermal unit
bu.	bushel
bull.	bulletin
bx., bxs.	box (es)
C	hundred
C.	centigrade, center
CAB	Civil Aeronautics Board
CAP	Civil Air Patrol
cap.	capital, capitalize, capital letter
cat.	catalog
C.B., CB	Citizens' Band (radio)
CBS, C.B.S.	Columbia Broadcasting System
cc, cc.	carbon copy
C/D, c/d	certificate of deposit
cf.	compare or see
c.f.m.	cubic feet per minute
ch.	chapter
C.I., CI	cast iron
c.i.f., C.I.F.	cost, insurance, and freight
Co.	company
c/o	in care of
c.o.d., C.O.D.	cash on delivery; collect on delivery
C.P.A., CPA	certified public accountant
C.P.S., CPS	certified professional secretary

cr.	credit, creditor
C.S.T., CST, c.s.t.	central standard time
cu.	cubic
cust.	customer
c.w.o.	cash with order
cwt.	hundredweight
D.C., DC	District of Columbia
d.c.	direct current
dep.	deputy, depot
dept.	department
dft.	draft
dis.	distance, distant, distribute
disc.	discount
div.	dividend, division, divisor
D/L	demand loan
dld.	delivered
dlvy.	delivery
doz.	dozen, dozens
Dr.	doctor
dr.	debit, debtor, dram
d.s.t.	daylight saving time
E.	east
ea.	each
ed., eds.	edition, editions
e.d.t.	eastern daylight time
e.g.	for example (*exempli gratia*)
enc.	enclosure, enclosed
Eng.	England, English
e.o.m.	end of month
Esq.	Esquire
est.	estimated, estate, established
E.S.T., EST, e.s.t.	eastern standard time
et al.	and others (*et alii, et aliae*)
etc.	and so forth (*et cetera*)
exc.	except, exception, excursion
exch.	exchange
ex div.	without a previously declared dividend
F	Fahrenheit
Fed.	Federal
ff.	folios, (and the) following (pages)
FIFO	first in, first out (accounting)
fig.	figure
FM	frequency modulation (radio)
f.o.b.	free on board
fol.	folio, following
FR	full-rate (telegrams and cables)
frt.	freight
ft.	foot, feet
fwd.	forward
FX, F.X.	foreign exchange
gal.	gallon
Gov.	governor
Govt., govt.	government
gr.	grain, gross
g.t.c., G.T.C.	good till cancelled (market)

Hon.	Honorable
hp.	horsepower
hr.	hour (s)
H.R.	House bill (with number)
hwy., hy.	highway
I.B.A.	Investment Bankers Association
ibid.	in the same place (*ibidem*)
I.B.M.	International Business Machines
i.e.	that is (*id est*)
ill.	illustrated, illustration, illustrator
in.	inch
Inc.	incorporated
incl.	inclosure, including, inclusive
INS, I.N.S.	International News Service
ins.	insurance, inches
Inst.	institution, institute
int.	interest, interior, international
IOU	I owe you
IQ	intelligence quotient
ital.	italic (type)
J.P.	justice of the peace
Jr.	junior
kt.	carat, kiloton
kw.	kilowatt
kw.-hr.	kilowatt-hour
l., ll.	line, lines
lat.	latitude
lb.	pound
lbs.	pounds
L/C, l/c	letter of credit
l.c.l.	less-than-carload lot
LIFO	last in, first out (accounting)
loc. cit.	in the place cited (*loco citato*)
long.	longitude
L.S.	place of the seal (*locus sigilli*)
Ltd.	limited
M	thousand
M.	Monsieur
MBS, M.B.S.	Mutual Broadcasting System
M.C.	Master of Ceremonies, Member of Congress
mdse.	merchandise
memo	memorandum
Messrs.	Messieurs (plural of *Mr.*), Gentlemen
mfg.	manufacturing
mfr.	manufacture, manufacturer
Mgr.	Manager
mi.	mile
min.	minute
misc.	miscellaneous
mkt.	market
Mlle.	mademoiselle
Mme.	madame
mo.	month
Mr.	mister
Mrs.	mistress

Ms.	Miss or Mrs. (title unknown or uncertain)
MS., MSS.	manuscript, manuscripts
M.S.T., MST, m.s.t.	mountain standard time
n/30	net in 30 days (invoice)
N., N, n.	North
N.A.M., NAM	National Association of Manufacturers
nat., natl.	national
NB	take notice (*note bene,* note well)
NBC, N.B.C.	National Broadcasting Company
N.E., NE.	northeast
No., Nos.	number, numbers
N.W., NW.	northwest
obs.	obsolete, observation
o/c	overcharge, over-the-counter (market)
OD	officer of the day
OK (OK'd, OK'ing, OK's)	approve, correct
op. cit.	in the work cited (*opere citato*)
orig.	origin, original, originally
oz.	ounce
p., pp.	page, pages
P.A., PA	press agent, public address (system)
pat.	patent, patented
payt.	payment
PBX	Private Branch (telephone) Exchange
pd.	paid
pfd.	preferred
pk.	peck
pkg., pkgs.	package, packages
pl.	plate, plural
p.m.	afternoon (*post meridiem*)
P.O.	post office, postal order
p.p.	parcel post, postpaid
pr.	pair, pairs
prem., pm.	premium
pro tem	temporarily (*pro tempore*)
P.S.	postscript (*post scriptum*)
P.S.T., PST, p.s.t.	Pacific standard time
pt.	pint, part
PTA	Parent-teacher association
P.W.D., PWD	Public Works Department
Q.E.D.	Which was to be proved (*quod erat demonstrandum*)
qr.	quarter, quire
qt.	quart
recd., rec'd	received
ref.	referee, reference, referred
Rep.	Representative, Republican, Republic
retd.	retained, returned
Rev.	Reverend
rm.	ream (paper), room
R.N.	registered nurse, Royal Navy
r.p.m.	revolutions per minute
RR.	railroad
R.R.	Rural Route

R.S.V.P., rsvp	reply, if you please (*répondez, s'il vous plaît*)
Rte.	Route
Rts.	rights (stock market)
Ry.	railway
S.	South, Senate bill (with number)
/S/	signed (before a copied signature)
S.A.	South America, Salvation Army, South Africa
S/D	sight draft
S/D-B/L	sight draft, bill of lading attached
S.E., SE.	southeast
sec., secy.	secretary
sec.	second, section
Sen., sen.	Senator, Senate
s.o.	seller's option
Soc., soc.	society
S O S	distress signal
sq. ft.	square foot
Sr.	Senior
S.R.O.	standing room only
ss	namely (*scilicet*)
St.	street
stet	let it stand (printing)
stk.	stock
Stk. Ex., St. Ex.	Stock Exchange
Supt.	superintendent
S.W., SW.	southwest
T., Tps.	township, townships
TB	tuberculosis
t.b.	trial balance
Treas.	treasurer, treasury
TV	television
TWX	teletypewriter exchange
U.	university, upper, union, unit
u.c., uc.	upper case
UFO	unidentified flying object
univ.	university, universally
U.P., UP	United Press
U.S.	United States
U.S.A.	United States of America
U.S.M.	United States Mail
U.S.O., USO	United Service Organizations
VHF	very high frequency
VIP	very important person (informal)
viz.	namely (*videlicit*)
vol.	volume
V.P.	Vice-President
vs.	against (*versus*)
v.v.	vice versa
W.	west
W.B., W/B, w.b.	waybill
whf.	wharf
whsle.	wholesale
w.i.	when issued
wk.	week
wt.	weight

yd.	yard
Y.M.C.A.	Young Men's Christian Association
yr.	year
Y.W.C.A.	Young Women's Christian Association

14-2. Academic Degrees and Their Abbreviations

B.A. *or* A.B	Bachelor of Arts
B.B.A.	Bachelor of Business Administration
B.C.	Bachelor of Chemistry
B.C.E.	Bachelor of Civil Engineering, Bachelor of Christian Education
B.C.L.	Bachelor of Civil Law
B.E.	Bachelor of Education
B.LL.	Bachelor of Laws
B.L.S.	Bachelor of Library Science
B.M.E.	Bachelor of Mechanical or of Mining Engineering or of Music Education
B.Mus.	Bachelor of Music
Ph.B.	Bachelor of Philosophy
B.S.	Bachelor of Science
M.A. *or* A.M.	Master of Arts
M.B.A.	Master of Business Administration
M.C.E.	Master of Civil Engineering
Ed.M.	Master of Education
M.S.	Master of Science
D.B.A.	Doctor of Business Administration
D.C.L.	Doctor of Civil Law
D.D.S.	Doctor of Dental Surgery, Doctor of Dental Science
D.D.	Doctor of Divinity
Ed.D.	Doctor of Education
Eng.D.	Doctor of Engineering
LL.D.	Doctor of Laws
Litt.D.	Doctor of Letters, Doctor of Literature
M.D.	Doctor of Medicine
Mus.D *or* Mus.Doc., *or* Mus.Dr.	Doctor of Music
Ph.D.	Doctor of Philosophy

14-3. Government Abbreviations

AEC	Atomic Energy Commission
ARC	American (National) Red Cross
CAA	Civil Aeronautics Administration
CAB	Civil Aeronautics Board
CCC	Commodity Credit Corporation
CIA	Central Intelligence Agency
CSC	Civil Service Commission
EIB	Export-Import Bank of Washington
FBI	Federal Bureau of Investigation
FCA	Farm Credit Administration
FCC	Federal Communications Commission
FCDA	Federal Civil Defense Administration
FDA	Food and Drug Administration
FDIC	Federal Deposit Insurance Corporation
FHA	Federal Housing Administration, Farmers Home Administration

FICA	Federal Insurance Contributions Act
FMC	Federal Maritime Commission
FNMA	Federal National Mortgage Association
FPC	Federal Power Commission
FR, F.R.	Federal Reserve
FRB, F.R.B.	Federal Reserve Bank or Board
FRS	Federal Reserve System
FSLIC	Federal Savings and Loan Insurance Corporation
FTC	Federal Trade Commission
ICC	Interstate Commerce Commission, Indian Claims Commission
IRS	Internal Revenue Service
MATS	Military Air Transport Service
NASA	National Aeronautics and Space Administration
NATO	North Atlantic Treaty Organization
NBS	National Bureau of Standards
NLRB	National Labor Relations Board
NSC	National Security Council
ODM	Office of Defense Mobilization
PHA	Public Housing Administration
PHS	Public Health Service
RRB	Railroad Retirement Board
ROTC, R.O.T.C.	Reserve Officers' Training Corps
SBA	Small Business Administration
SEC	Securities and Exchange Commission
SSA	Social Security Administration
SSS	Selective Service System
TVA	Tennessee Valley Authority
USA	United States Army
USAF	United States Air Force
USCG	United States Coast Guard
USES	United States Employment Service
USIA	United States Information Agency
USMC	United States Marine Corps
USN	United States Navy
USNR	United States Naval Reserve
VA	Veterans Administration
WAC	Women's Army Corps

14-4. Abbreviations of United Nations Affiliates

FAO	Food and Agricultural Organization
IADB	Inter-American Defense Board
ICAO	International Civil Aviation Organization
ILO	International Labor Organization
ITU	International Telecommunication Union
UN	United Nations
UNA	United Nations Assembly
UNESCO	United Nations Educational, Scientific, and Cultural Organization
UPU	Universal Postal Union
WHO	World Health Organization
WMO	World Metereological Organization

14-5. State, District, and Territory Names; Abbreviations; Capitals

The following table shows the names of the states, districts, and territories of the United States; the standard abbreviations of the names; the new two-letter abbreviations that are used only with ZIP Codes; and the capital cities.

NAME	STANDARD ABBREVIATION	TWO-LETTER ABBREVIATION	CAPITAL
Alabama	Ala.	AL	Montgomery
Alaska	Alaska	AK	Juneau
Arizona	Ariz.	AZ	Phoenix
Arkansas	Ark.	AR	Little Rock
California	Calif.	CA	Sacramento
Canal Zone	C. Z.	CZ	
Colorado	Colo.	CO	Denver
Connecticut	Conn.	CT	Hartford
Delaware	Del.	DE	Dover
District of Columbia	D. C.	DC	Washington
Florida	Fla.	FL	Tallahassee
Georgia	Ga.	GA	Atlanta
Guam	Guam	GU	Agana
Hawaii	Hawaii	HI	Honolulu
Idaho	Idaho	ID	Boise
Illinois	Ill.	IL	Springfield
Indiana	Ind.	IN	Indianapolis
Iowa	Iowa	IA	Des Moines
Kansas	Kans.	KS	Topeka
Kentucky	Ky.	KY	Frankfort
Louisiana	La.	LA	Baton Rouge
Maine	Maine	ME	Augusta
Maryland	Md.	MD	Annapolis
Massachusetts	Mass.	MA	Boston
Michigan	Mich.	MI	Lansing
Minnesota	Minn.	MN	St. Paul
Mississippi	Miss.	MS	Jackson
Missouri	Mo.	MO	Jefferson City
Montana	Mont.	MT	Helena
Nebraska	Nebr.	NE	Lincoln
Nevada	Nev.	NV	Carson City
New Hampshire	N. H.	NH	Concord
New Jersey	N. J.	NJ	Trenton
New Mexico	N. Mex.	NM	Santa Fe
New York	N. Y.	NY	Albany

NAME	STANDARD ABBREVIATION	TWO-LETTER ABBREVIATION	CAPITAL
North Carolina	N. C.	NC	Raleigh
North Dakota	N. Dak.	ND	Bismarck
Ohio	Ohio	OH	Columbus
Oklahoma	Okla.	OK	Oklahoma City
Oregon	Oreg.	OR	Salem
Pennsylvania	Pa.	PA	Harrisburg
Puerto Rico	P. R.	PR	San Juan
Rhode Island	R. I.	RI	Providence
South Carolina	S. C.	SC	Columbia
South Dakota	S. Dak.	SD	Pierre
Tennessee	Tenn.	TN	Nashville
Texas	Tex.	TX	Austin
Utah	Utah	UT	Salt Lake City
Vermont	Vt.	VT	Montpelier
Virgin Islands	V. I.	VI	Charlotte Amalie
Virginia	Va.	VA	Richmond
Washington	Wash.	WA	Olympia
West Virginia	W. Va.	WV	Charleston
Wisconsin	Wis.	WI	Madison
Wyoming	Wyo.	WY	Cheyenne

14-6. Canadian Names, Abbreviations, and Capitals

The following table shows the names of the Canadian provinces, the standard abbreviations of the names, the new two-letter abbreviations of the names, and the capitals of the provinces.

NAME	STANDARD ABBREVIATION	TWO-LETTER ABBREVIATION	CAPITAL
Alberta	Alta.	AB	Edmonton
British Columbia	B.C.	BC	Victoria
Manitoba	Man.	MB	Winnipeg
New Brunswick	N.B.	NB	Fredericton
Newfoundland	Newf./Nfld.	NF	St. John's
Northwest Territories	N.W.Ter.	NT	Yellowknife
Nova Scotia	N.S.	NS	Halifax
Ontario	Ont.	ON	Toronto
Prince Edward Island	P.E.I.	PE	Charlottetown
Quebec	Que.	PQ	Quebec
Saskatchewan	Sask.	SK	Regina
Yukon Territory		YT	Whitehorse
Labrador	Lab.	LB	*none*

14-7. Data Processing Abbreviations

ADP	automatic data processing
ALGOL	algorithmic oriented language
COBOL	common business oriented language
EAM	electrical accounting machine
EDP	electronic data processing
EOF	end of file
FORTRAN	formula translation (procedure oriented programming language)
IDP	integrated data processing
I/O	input-output
MICR	magnetic ink character recognition
OCR	optical character recognition

14-8. Symbols

Suggestions are shown within parentheses for typing those symbols that are not standardized on all typewriters.

addition	$\not{/}$	(diagonal, backspace, hyphen)
and (ampersand)	$\&$	
at	@	
caret (omission)	work the/project	(diagonal)
cent, cents	¢	
chemistry symbols	H_2O	(use variable line spacer)
degree	70°	(use variable line spacer and lower case o)
ditto	"	(quotation mark)
division	÷	(colon, backspace, hyphen)
English pound	£	(upper case L, backspace, variable line spacer, hyphen)
equal sign	=	(hyphen, backspace, variable line spacer, hyphen)
exponent (superior number)	12^2	(variable line spacer and numeral)
feet	16'	(apostrophe)

fraction (made)	5/8	(diagonal)
inches	9"	(quotation mark)
minus	–	(hyphen)
multiplication	x	(lower case x)
number (before a figure)	#	
paragraph sign	ℙ	(shift lock, strike I, **backspace** slightly, strike P)
percent	%	
pound (after a figure)	#	
seconds	"	(quotation mark)
signed (before a copied signature)	/S/	(diagonal, S, diagonal)

The Mail

Most large firms have two kinds of mail: (1) mail within the organization, called *interoffice mail,* and (2) mail to and from other firms and persons. Interoffice mail may be handled in a variety of ways, according to the wishes of the individual firm. Mail to and from correspondents is handled according to the many services of the United States Post Office, all of which are governed by specific laws and regulations. Office personnel who handle mail should familiarize themselves with post office laws, regulations, and procedures.

15-1. Incoming Mail

1. Sorting is the first step in the handling of incoming mail. Letters marked "Personal" are separated from the firm or company mail. The latter may then be divided into the following types of mail:

   a. First-class business letters and telegrams
   b. Circulars and advertising materials
   c. Newspapers and magazines
   d. Packages

2. Letters marked "Personal" are delivered unopened to the persons to whom they are addressed.

3. All other mail should then be opened, time-stamped, and inspected for signatures, enclosures, and complete addresses.

4. Notations should be made on letters, when necessary, to call attention to any apparent omissions. The envelopes should be attached to the letters to which they belong. Some firms clip all envelopes to the original letters.

5. Next, the mail is distributed. The method of distribution varies with the type and size of the firm.

15-2. Outgoing Mail

1. Every letter should be considered as part of a unit of correspondence consisting of the original letter, the required number of carbons, the matching envelope, and the necessary enclosures. It is the responsibility of the typist to see that every unit is complete. This involves checking to see that the letter is properly signed and given final disposition.

2. Inaccurate addresses delay delivery of the mail. To help eliminate errors in envelope addressing, the typist should follow these steps:

15

Lowrey, Inc.
432 Yeardly Rd.
Washington, D.C. 20016

```
Mr. Ralph Estes
R.R. 4, Box 267
Carmen, OK  73726
```

Greenhills Landscape Service
127 HILLTOP LANE
SAN FRANCISCO, CALIFORNIA 94141

```
Mrs. Virginia Griffin
Wilberford, Inc.
42 Los Palmos Drive
San Francisco, Calif.  94127
```

allan
silver company
666 North High Street
Buffalo, New York 14202

```
Acme Jewelry Co.
Attention Mr. John Boggio
301 Hartford Avenue
Buffalo, NY  14223
```

15

15-a. Acceptable Styles of Envelope Addresses

a. Verify the address before it is typed. Include in the envelope address the same information that appears in the inside address of the letter unless additional directions are necessary.

b. Type accurately and spell correctly.

c. Regardless of the size of the envelope, type the address so that it will be attractively arranged and well balanced. On a small envelope, begin the address 2 inches from the top and 2½ inches from the left edge of the envelope. On a large envelope, begin the address 2½ inches from the top and 4 inches from the left edge.

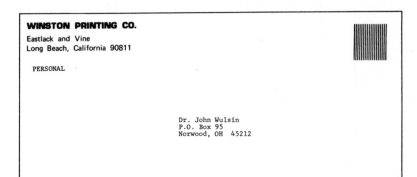

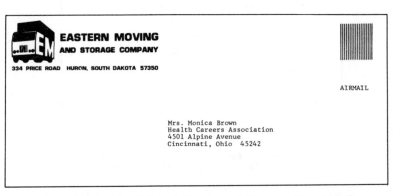

15-a. Acceptable Styles of Envelope Addresses (Concluded)

d. Single-space the address, regardless of the number of lines required. Even if no street address is given, type the city, state, and ZIP Code on one line.

e. Include a title for the person whose name appears on the envelope.

f. Use a street address whenever possible.

g. Type the name of the city rather than the word CITY; include the ZIP Code on all domestic mail. (See pages 131 and 132 for a list of the two-letter state abbreviations that may be used with ZIP Codes.)

h. Avoid symbols or abbreviations unless they are required in specific instances.

i. Write out *North, East, South,* and *West* when they are part of the street address. However, it is sometimes permissible to abbreviate these directional words to improve the balance of the address lines.

    319 North Francis Avenue   286 Lincoln Street, East

**15-b. Proper Arrangement of a Letter and
Its Envelope on the Dictator's Desk**

j. Use compound sectional directions after names to indicate separate sections of the city.

3619 Norwood Avenue, N.W.   2178 - 97th Street, S.E.
or   *or*
3619 Norwood Avenue, NW.   2178 - 97th Street, SE.

k. Place any special reference of a personal, confidential, or routine nature a triple space below the return address and three spaces from the left edge of the envelope.

l. Place a notation involving special services requested (special delivery, special handling, airmail, etc.) below the stamp and at least three line spaces above the address.

m. If the sender's address is not printed on the envelope, type it in the upper left corner of the envelope.

n. Recheck the address before mailing the letter.

3. Insert the finished letter under the flap of the envelope. Place the completed unit—the dictated letter and its envelope, the enclosures, and the required number of carbon copies—on the dictator's desk in readable position for signing. When the mail is not signed promptly, or when the context is of a highly confidential nature, the letter may be placed face downward, or each unit may be enclosed in an individual folder.

4. The final step in the preparation of a letter for mailing is the folding. This should be done in such a way that the letter will not only fit in the envelope but also can be removed and opened conveniently. The method of folding depends upon the size and type of envelope.

5. To fold a letter to fit in a small envelope and to insert it into the envelope, follow the steps in the illustration shown below.

Small (Nos. 6¾ and 6¼)

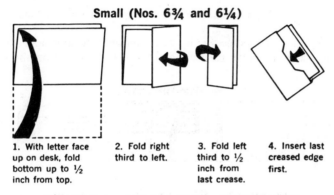

1. With letter face up on desk, fold bottom up to ½ inch from top.

2. Fold right third to left.

3. Fold left third to ½ inch from last crease.

4. Insert last creased edge first.

15-c. Folding a Letter to Fit in a Small Envelope

6. To fold a letter to fit in a large envelope and to insert it into the envelope, follow the steps in the illustration shown below.

Large (Nos. 10, 9, and 7¾)

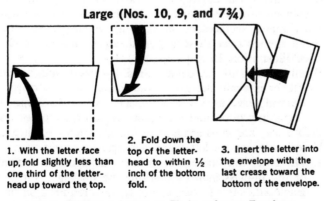

1. With the letter face up, fold slightly less than one third of the letterhead up toward the top.

2. Fold down the top of the letterhead to within ½ inch of the bottom fold.

3. Insert the letter into the envelope with the last crease toward the bottom of the envelope.

15-d. Folding a Letter to Fit in a Large Envelope

7. To fold a letter to fit in a window envelope and to insert it into the envelope, follow the steps in the illustration shown below.

Window (Letter)

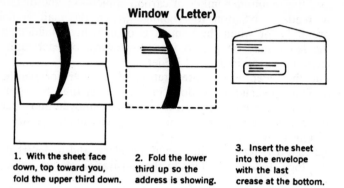

1. With the sheet face down, top toward you, fold the upper third down.

2. Fold the lower third up so the address is showing.

3. Insert the sheet into the envelope with the last crease at the bottom.

15-e. Folding a Letter to Fit in a Large Window Envelope

8. To fold an invoice to fit in a window envelope and to insert it into the envelope, follow the steps in the illustration shown below.

Window (Invoice)

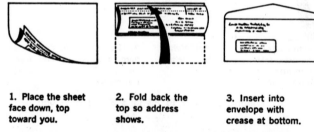

1. Place the sheet face down, top toward you.

2. Fold back the top so address shows.

3. Insert into envelope with crease at bottom.

15-f. Folding an Invoice to Fit in a Window Envelope

9. When a large number of envelopes must be sealed without the use of a mechanical device, it is expedient to arrange a series of envelopes face downward on the desk in such a way that only the gummed surfaces of the flaps are exposed. Next run a moistened sponge over these gummed edges and seal each envelope. (See Illustration 15-g, page 141.)

10. When stamps are to be attached by hand and no commercial moistener is available, a wet pad made from a strip of cotton or gauze will serve as a substitute. The sealed envelopes should be arranged in groups, and the stamps separated into horizontal strips before they are moistened. (See Illustration 15-h, page 141.)

11. If desirable, mail a letter and a parcel as a unit.

a. The letter may be enclosed in a package sent second-, third-, or fourth-class mail by marking the package "First-Class Mail Enclosed." In addition to the postage required on the package, the first-class postage is placed on the outside of the package.

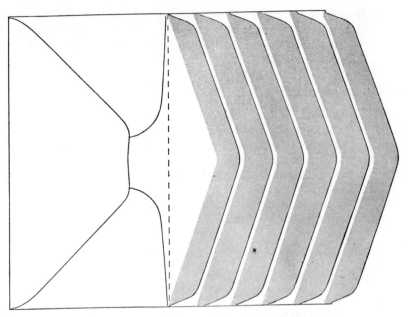

15-g. Envelopes Arranged for Hand Sealing

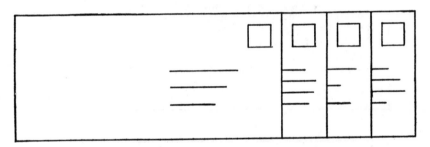

15-h. Envelopes Arranged for Hand Stamping

b. The letter may be attached to the outside of the package. The envelope containing first-class mail may be marked "First Class" or "Letter Enclosed." The envelope must be addressed the same as the parcel. In addition to the postage placed on the parcel, stamps covering first-class postage are placed on the envelope.

c. Combination envelopes or containers having separate partitions for a letter and mail of another class may be used for mailing together two classes of mail.

12. Mailing lists, if arranged on 3″ x 5″ cards, will be corrected by the Post Office Department for a stated fee. Lists used by members of Congress and federal agencies are corrected without charge.

13. Senders of undeliverable publications and undeliverable third- and fourth-class mail will be notified of such fact upon payment of the specified fee and the proper endorsement, such as "Return postage guaranteed," etc.

15-3. Government Postal Cards

1. The United States postal card, regulation size 5½ x 3¼ inches, is used for many types of business messages. While sales notices, adjustments, claims, routine messages and announcements, etc., may be sent on postal cards, dunning statements will not be accepted by the United States Post Office unless they are under sealed cover.

2. To conserve space, the inside address is omitted. Single spacing is used for the message.

August 8, 19--

Dear Member:

The second meeting of the AMS Chapter Profile Committee will take place at the Metropolitan Inn on Monday evening, August 15, at eight o'clock. The final design of the questionnaire will be discussed. I hope to see you there!

Alfred Henderson

Alfred Henderson
Chairman

Alfred Henderson
341 Circle Tower
5 East Market Street
Indianapolis, IN 46204

Mr. John Roman
608 East Ninth Street
Indianapolis, IN 46202

15-i. Message and Address Typed on a Postal Card

3. Individual business messages typed on government postal cards should carry the date and a signature.

4. Postal cards are available not only in "singles" but also in sheets of 40 for use in printing. The sheets, which must be cut to regulation size, are sold in cases that may be broken for sale to printers.

5. Stamped envelopes and government postal cards that have been spoiled in addressing are not a total loss. These should be accumulated and returned to the post office for redemption. Redemption is made in postage stamps, stamped envelopes, or postal cards, but not in cash.

15-4. Interoffice Communications

1. Interoffice communications—exchanges of ideas between individuals, departments, or branch offices of one organization—are either written or spoken.

2. Spoken messages are executed by means of the extension telephone, the conference phone, closed-circuit TV, and various types of intercommunication systems.

3. Written interoffice messages should be typed on specially prepared forms. These forms vary in size, color, and quality of stock from the regular stationery.

    a. The inside address, the salutation, and the complimentary close are omitted.

INTEROFFICE MEMORANDUM

CENTRAL NATIONAL BANK

Cincinnati, OH 45202

TO: Brighton Office

FROM: Alfred Noyes, Downtown Office

DATE: 4/16/--

SUBJECT: Cash Reserve Plan

The cash reserve plan for preferred customers will be initiated September 15. Please send all applications to the attention of Mr. Carl Kotter, Director, Cash Reserve Plan, Downtown Office.

Applications will be processed promptly. Branch offices will receive daily lists of approved customers and the limits set on their reserve accounts.

er

15-j. Interoffice Communication Form

b. The date may be written in short form.

4-16-70   4/16/70

c. Since the form carries the name of the person dictating the message, it need not have a signature when it is sent to a group; but it is good form to initial messages intended for individuals.

15-5. Postal Information

1. The understanding of postal regulations facilitates the efficient handling of mail. Every office should be provided with the latest edition of *The Postal Manual,* which contains the regulations and internal instructions governing the operation of the postal service.

a. Chapter 1 contains regulations pertaining to the use of domestic mail service.

b. Chapter 2 contains corresponding regulations pertaining to the use of international mail service.

2. Purchasers of *The Postal Manual* are furnished periodic loose-leaf supplements for an indefinite period.

3. *The Postal Manual* may be obtained from the Superintendent of Documents, U.S. Government Printing Office, Washington, D.C. 20402.

4. Smaller publications in which basic postal information is abstracted are also available from local post offices.

15-6. Classification of Mail

1. First-class matter

a. Letters and postal cards.

b. Airmail not to exceed 7 ounces.

c. Business reply mail.

d. All matter wholly or partly in writing, including original type-written material and carbon copies.

e. Publications or parcels which would ordinarily be classified as second-, third-, or fourth-class but which may be sent first-class. Local post office officials can supply details on this topic.

2. Second-class matter

a. Newspapers and periodicals bearing notice of entry as second-class matter.

b. Rates will vary according to the weight and type of publication and the mailing distance.

3. Third-class matter

a. Books and catalogs of 24 pages or more with at least 22 printed pages.

  b. Proof sheets and corrected proof sheets with related manuscript copy.

  c. Bills or statements of account produced by photographic or mechanical process when presented in 20 or more identical copies.

  d. Merchandise weighing no more than 16 ounces.

  e. Hotel and steamship keys (mailed uncovered) that carry instructions to return and a statement guaranteeing payment of postage due.

  f. Seeds, cuttings, bulbs, roots, and plants.

  g. All other mailable matter within the weight limitations (up to but not including 16 ounces) not included as first- or second-class mail.

4. Fourth-class matter (parcel post)

  a. Merchandise, printed matter, mailable live animals, and all other matter not included as first-, second-, or third-class mail.

  b. Each addressed piece must weigh 16 ounces or more.

  c. Since parcel-post rates change according to the distance each piece is to be sent, as well as according to the weight, consult *The Postal Manual* or check with your local post office.

5. Airmail

  a. Mail of all classes, except that which may be damaged by low temperatures or high altitudes, is accepted for airmail.

  b. Airmail may weigh up to 70 pounds.

  c. Airmail is limited to 100 inches in combined length and girth.

  d. Postage is charged on airmail (except postal cards) according to class of mail.

15-7. Special Mail Services

1. Certificate of mailing

  a. Certificates of mailing furnish evidence of mailing only. No receipt is obtained from the addressee upon delivery and the certificate does not ensure the article against loss or damage.

  b. The fee is based on the number of pieces of mail described on the original certificate.

2. Certified mail

  a. Certified mail provides a means of proof that first-class mail has been delivered. The sender is provided a receipt, and a record of delivery is maintained at the post office of the addressee for six months.

  b. Certified mail does not provide payment to the sender if the item is lost.

c. A fee for the certified mail service, in addition to postage, may be paid by ordinary postage stamps, meter stamps, or permit imprints.

d. For a small additional fee, a return receipt may be requested.

e. For payment of a small fee, restricted delivery will restrict the delivery of mail to the addressee.

3. C.O.D. service

a. By means of c.o.d. (collect-on-delivery) service, the buyer need not pay for goods until he receives them, but the seller can make sure that he will be paid.

b. When a package is sent c.o.d., the usual postage plus additional postage covering the fee charged for the c.o.d. service must be placed on the package by the sender.

c. The total of the c.o.d. charges will be collected by the post office before the package is turned over to the addressee. The buyer is not permitted to examine the contents before accepting the parcel.

d. The maximum amount that may be collected on any one parcel is $200.

4. Insurance

a. It is possible to insure third- or fourth-class mail or airmail containing third- or fourth-class matter against loss or damage not exceeding $200 on any one parcel by the payment of a fee in addition to the usual postage.

b. Insurance fees are based on the value of the contents.

c. For a small fee, a return receipt may be requested for a parcel insured for more than $10.

d. For payment of a small fee, restricted delivery will restrict the delivery of mail to the addressee.

5. Registry

a. All mailable matter paid at first-class rates may be registered by the prepayment of a fee in addition to the regular postage.

b. The Post Office Department is held liable for the safe delivery of registered mail, but the liability is limited to the declared value that the sender places on the registered mail.

c. Upon the payment of a special fee, the sender of registered mail may demand a return receipt. This receipt, signed by the one to whom the mail was addressed, will show that the mail actually was received.

d. For payment of a small fee, restricted delivery will restrict the delivery of mail to the addressee.

6. Special delivery

    a. When a letter marked "Special Delivery" is received at a post office in the city of the addressee, it is delivered as quickly as possible without interrupting the normal work flow of the post office.

    b. Special delivery service is available for all classes of mail. The rate depends upon the weight and class of the package.

    c. A 45-cent special delivery stamp or the equivalent value in stamps plus the regular postage will ensure the special delivery of first-class and airmail matter not weighing more than two pounds. A larger fee is charged for heavier first-class and airmail matter.

    d. For all other classes of mail not weighing more than two pounds, the fee is 65 cents; a larger fee is charged for heavier matter.

    e. Each piece of mail should be marked "Special Delivery" above the name of the addressee.

7. Special handling

    a. Special handling, often confused with special delivery, applies to third- and fourth-class matter only and means that the package will be taken out of its regular class and sent by first class to the addressee. This special service ends, however, at the final post office. The package is then delivered on the first regular trip.

    b. Special handling must be used for all parcels that require special attention in handling, transportation, and delivery.

    c. The special handling fee is paid in addition to the regular fourth-class postage. Special handling fees vary with the weight of the parcel.

    d. The package should be marked "Special Handling."

15-8. Nonmail Services

1. Money orders

    a. The Post Office Department provides for the sale of domestic and international money orders as a means of transmitting money.

    b. The maximum amount for which a postal money order can be drawn is $100. If a person wishes to send a larger amount as a remittance, he must purchase two or more orders. For example, a remittance of $201 would require three postal money orders. A small fee is charged for this service.

2. Nonpostal stamps and bonds—internal revenue stamps, migratory bird-hunting stamps, and United States savings stamps and bonds —are also offered for sale by post offices.

The Telephone

The ubiquitous telephone is one of the basic communication devices of the business world. Anyone who works in an office should know how to place and receive calls correctly and should be familiar with the important extra services offered by telephone companies.

16-1. Incoming Local Calls

1. Handle incoming calls with promptness and courtesy since the manner of answering calls may create a favorable or unfavorable impression upon the person making the call.
2. As a matter of efficiency and economy when answering the phone, identify yourself or your firm immediately by saying:

   > "Keenan Motor Company"
   > "The Chromite Oil Company, Service Department"
   > "Dr. Murphy's office, Miss Eagen speaking"
   > "555-3268" *or* "Scott's residence"

3. You may adopt a plan of answering incoming calls with greetings. Many stores, hotels, theaters, and other business firms do this.

   > "Good Morning, Mercury Theater"
   > "Commonwealth Hotel, Good Evening"

4. Get the name of the person or firm making the call, obtain the purpose of the message, and give such information as will satisfy the calling party.
5. Keep a pad and pencil at every telephone for making notations concerning calls. To avoid delay and misunderstanding, repeat any messages, including telephone numbers. Spell out the caller's name. Offices should provide interoffice forms for recording appointments, messages, orders, and other business.

16-2. Outgoing Local Calls

1. Obtain the correct number. When in doubt, consult the directory furnished by the telephone company. There are two sources for securing numbers: the subscribers' alphabetic directory and the Yellow Pages. If the name cannot be located in either source, call "Information" and ask for the number.
2. To place an outside call directly, secure a dial tone on an outside line and dial the seven digits of the number. If a wrong number is reached, apologize, then break the connection and dial the correct number.

3. To place a call through a switchboard (PBX), follow one of the procedures given below. (The first procedure is the usual one.)

    a. Raise the receiver; listen for the special dial tone (distinguishable from the regular outside dial tone); dial a code number (usually "9") to get the outside dial tone; dial the number. If no outside lines are available, you will hear a special busy signal. Most offices with extension telephones use this system.

    b. Some systems require the caller to raise the receiver, ask the PBX operator for an outside line, and then dial his number.

4. In case of emergency, look for the required emergency number on the inside front cover of the telephone directory. If you cannot look up the number in an emergency, dial "O" (Operator). Be sure to state your name and address and the nature of the emergency if you cannot remain on the line.

16-3. Long Distance Calls

1. Long distance calls may be either station-to-station or person-to-person calls.

    a. A station-to-station call is made when the person who is calling is willing to speak to anyone who answers the telephone at the called point.

    b. A person-to-person call should be made when the caller wishes to talk with a certain person at the number. Although person-to-person calls are slightly more expensive than station-to-station calls, a person-to-person call may be more economical if the person is difficult to locate.

2. Rates for long distance telephone calls vary according to the distance, the type of service, the time of day, the day of the week, and the time consumed in holding the conversation.

3. Long distance calls may be dialed direct or may be completed with the aid of a long distance operator. Direct-distance dialing enables one to place a call direct as easily and as simply as dialing a local telephone number. For direct-distance dialing, one must know the correct area code and telephone number.

    If you do not know the number and if the destination of the call is in your own Numbering Plan Area (see Figure 16-a), dial 1-555-1212 for information. If you do not know the number and if the destination of the call is *not* in your own Numbering Plan Area (see Figure 16-a), dial "1" and the area code for the city to which you are calling and *then* dial 555-1212. There is no charge for a directory assistance call.

16

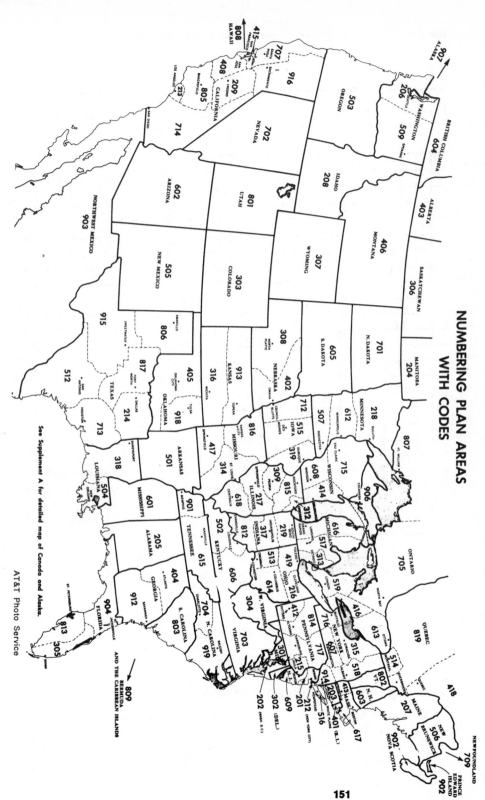

NUMBERING PLAN AREAS WITH CODES

16-a. Telephone Area Codes in the United States and Canada

AT&T Photo Service

See Supplement A for detailed map of Canada and Alaska.

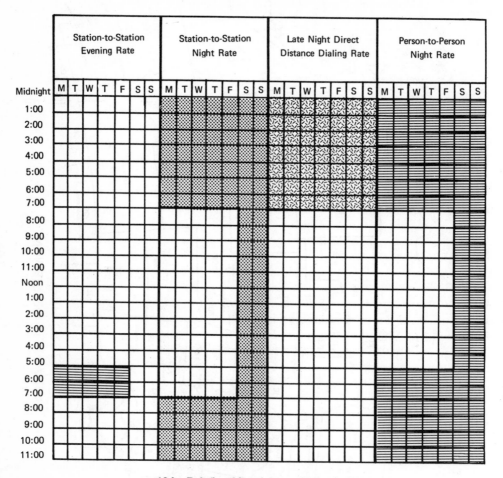

16-b. Relationship of Long Distance Rates
The shaded areas represent lower-rate times. The times are
the local times at the origin of the calls.

4. When a person wishes to have the charges reversed (paid for at
the other end of the line), that fact should be made known at
the time of placing the call. The person called must agree to
accept these charges before the call is completed.

16-4. Special Telephone Services

1. An appointment call may be placed when a particular person is
wanted at a specific time. In addition to the specific time at which
the call should be put through, the long distance operator is given
the same information as for any other person-to-person call.

2. Conference service offered by telephone companies enables group conversations to be established. This makes it possible for Mr. A in Milwaukee, Mr. B in New York, Mr. C in Dallas, and Mr. D in Los Angeles to get into direct communication with one another at the same time. Dial the operator for this service.

3. Some other special telephone services which are available are as follows:

> Automatic dialing devices
> Wide area telephone service (bulk rates for long distance calls within a certain area)
> Mobile telephone service (telephones in vehicles)
> Data communications

16-5. Telephone Etiquette

1. Personality can be reflected over the telephone as easily as in face-to-face conversations. In telephone conversations, however, the tone of voice, the manner of speaking, and the selection of words alone convey personality.

2. Correct telephone habits aid in making good impressions. It pays to have a good telephone personality.

a. Answer calls promptly.
b. Identify yourself at once.
c. Speak slowly, clearly, and distinctly.
d. Cultivate a cheerful tone of voice.
e. Be as courteous over the phone as you would be face to face.
f. Offer to take a message.
g. Record any calls received during the absence of an employer.
h. Listen attentively to the person with whom you are speaking.
i. Concentrate on your telephone conversation.
j. Be sure that information given over the telephone is authentic.
k. Plan your conversation before you begin to talk.
l. If a mistake is made in dialing, apologize to the person who was disturbed.
m. Consult the directory for numbers. Do not rely on your memory.
n. Pronounce each digit separately in giving numbers to the operator.
o. Don't keep people waiting.
p. Leave a pleasant feeling when you close a conversation.

16-6. The Telephone Voice

When people talk face-to-face, the impressions formed are based on many factors. When they talk by telephone, the entire personality must be projected by the voice alone. If the person speaking on the telephone projects a pleasant personality, the firm gains stature in the mind of the party on the other end of the line.

Any mechanical means of communication is, by its very nature, impersonal. The tone of voice, precision of punctuation, and inflection that serve well when supported by gestures and facial expressions may not stand alone when stripped of that support by the telephone. Listen to other voices on the telephone. Those who project the best images speak more slowly and more clearly than is required in normal conversation. If you listen carefully, you can detect a conscious effort to be understood clearly.

The real telephone charmers are those who speak slowly and distinctly enough to overcome the mechanical impersonality of the telephone—but still manage to sound warm and cordial. A good way to practice is to pronounce numbers so they are easily understood without adopting an affected pronunciation. Remember! A little extra emphasis, a little extra projection, a little extra personality—but not affectation.

Telegrams

Telegraphic services provide a rapid means of written communication. Because of the speed with which telegrams are transmitted, they induce a feeling of urgency and importance, thereby gaining immediate attention.

Telegrams are used to place, trace, change, confirm, or cancel orders; to register complaints, make adjustments and/or cancellations, and close deals; to revive inactive accounts and collect delinquent accounts; to transmit money; to stimulate selling campaigns; to secure and give credit information; to make hotel reservations; and to convey business and personal greetings.

17-1. Kinds of Telegraphic Communications

1. Domestic services

    a. The standard, full-rate, fast service telegram (FR) is based on a message of 15 words or less in text. For a longer message, a charge is made for each additional word.
    b. The overnight telegram (NL) is accepted up to 12 midnight for delivery the next morning. Rates are substantially lower than those for the full-rate telegram. The overnight telegram is based on a message of 100 words in text. For a longer message, a charge is made for each additional word.

2. International services

    a. The full-rate cablegram (FR) is standard service at the full rate.
    b. The letter cablegram (LT) is an overnight plain-language message based on a 22-word minimum.
    c. The name, address, and signature are counted and charged for in all international services.

3. Special types of communications

    a. Private wire systems, also called *closed-circuit telegraph*, consist of the leasing of telegraphic circuits and equipment for private wire use. The systems vary in size from the simple circuit between two points with a machine called a *teleprinter* at each end for direct and unlimited service for specifically contracted hours, to the custom-built automatic systems installed for national concerns. For the latter, mechanized centers, or computer centers, automatically flash across the country in much the same way as the telegraph company operates its circuits.

17

b. Desk-Fax or Telefax unit equipment may be installed in customers' offices, which are assigned call letters, to facilitate the sending and receiving of telegrams. The messages, typed on special forms, are sent and received in picture form. Since transmission is automatic, no special skill in operation is required. (See Illustration 17-b, page 158, for the correct form to follow in typing a Telefax message.)

c. Teletypewriter services are handled through teletypewriters, which are machines operated similarly to typewriters but are reserved for wire communications only. They provide direct, accurate, and speedy communications between distant firms.

Two-way communications can be handled with the teletypewriter. One operator may type a question and receive an immediate answer, or several firms through their specially trained operators may engage in continual conversation on the teletypewriters.

17-2. Preparing Telegrams

1. If a telegram is sent by a person who goes to an office of Western Union, he fills out a standard telegraph blank that is ruled for handwriting. This blank would rarely be used for a typewritten telegram because the vertical spacing of the rules does not correspond to the vertical spacing of a typewriter.

2. If a telegram is transmitted to a Western Union office by telephone or teleprinter, type one or more copies of the message on plain paper for the files. On the copy, show the following information: (1) the class of service specified, (2) the account to be charged if other than that of the sender, (3) the date and time the message was filed, (4) the name and address of the recipient, (5) the message itself, (6) the sender's name and possibly his title, and (7) the reference initials of the typist. The form used in typing these data varies among offices. (See Illustration 17-a, page 157, for one acceptable form.)

3. Type a Telefax message with all capital letters or with lower case, capitalizing only where necessary.

4. A telegram on a regular telegraph blank will be sent as a fast telegram unless the sender places a check mark in the box entitled "Overnight Telegram." A Telefax message will be sent as a fast message if the letters "FR" are typed on the blank or if no letters indicating the type of service appear. If the message is to be sent as an overnight message, the letters "NL" should be typed on the blank on the line immediately following the line for the call letters of the sender.

5. The abbreviation "PD." or the abbreviation "COL." should be written on a telegraph blank in the box provided to indicate

TELEGRAM

Overnight Telegram

December 10, 19--, 2 p.m.

Roy C. Evans, Production Manager
Louisville Industries, Inc.
321 West Broadway
Louisville, Kentucky

Arriving Thursday at noon. Ask Messrs. Downing, Franklin, and
Norris to attend a meeting at two o'clock. We must discuss
the progress made up to now on the Hammerhill order. We must
make plans to speed up the work from now on. Unless the work
is completed by March 31, we will not receive a repeat order.
Ask Messrs. Downing, Franklin, and Norris to study the problem
and have concrete suggestions to offer at the meeting.

Arnold Freeman, Vice-President
Henderson-Rowen, Inc.

rd

17-a. File Copy of Telegram on Plain Paper

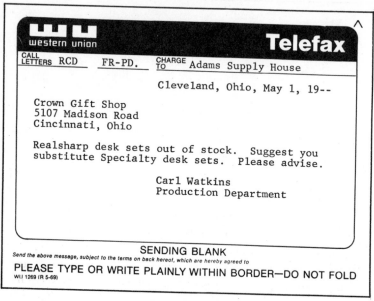

17-b. Telefax

whether the message is to be sent prepaid or collect. These same abbreviations should be typed on a Telefax message immediately after the indication of the class of service.

6. In both kinds of messages (regular telegram and Telefax), the name of the account to be charged should be indicated in the proper box.

7. Omit the titles *Mr.* and *Messrs.*, but include *Miss* or *Mrs.*

8. Insert the necessary punctuation marks. In their ordinary sense, they are transmitted without cost.

9. Type the required number of copies. Current practice that is fairly frequent is to type a copy on plain paper. Copies may be used for mail confirmation, for filing, and for billing purposes.

10. Omit unnecessary words, but do not sacrifice clarity.

11. Do not divide a word at the end of a line. Carry the complete word to the next line.

12. Avoid the use of contractions and abbreviations.

13. Spell in full *east, west, north,* and *south.*

14. Check the accuracy of spelling.

15. Provide only one copy with a mailing list if the same telegram is to be sent to more than one person or firm. The telegraph company will prepare and transmit a copy to every addressee. There is no limit to the size of the mailing list. This type of telegram is known as a *multi-gram.*

16. When specific information pertaining to rates, codes, and special services is required, consult your local telegraph company.

17-3. Counting Chargeable Words

1. The cost of a telegram is based upon a count of all figures, letters, and words used in the text of the telegram. For international services, the count also includes the address and the signature.

2. In domestic service, the common punctuation marks are not counted or charged for. These marks include the period, comma, colon, semicolon, hyphen, dash, parentheses, question mark, quotation marks, and apostrophe. In international service, a charge is made for marks of punctuation.

3. Any standard dictionary word in the eight admitted languages (English, German, Spanish, Italian, French, Dutch, Portuguese, and Latin) is counted as one word in all other languages. In cablegrams the standard word in any of the eight admitted languages is limited to 15 letters.

4. Code words (standard English words used arbitrarily) and cipher words (groups of miscellaneous letters) may be used in lieu of phrases or sentences to effect economy and secrecy. The charge for a message in cipher is based on the rate of five letters to a word. Thus, *lalfak* would be counted as two words.

5. The abbreviation of a single word is counted as a full word.

6. Common abbreviations without spaces between letters, as *c.o.d.,* *f.o.b., a.m.,* and *p.m.,* are counted as one word for every five characters.

7. Each initial is ordinarily counted as one word; as, *J. C. Smith* (three words). But when initials are written together, they are counted as one word for each five letters.

8. The following symbols should be written out and sent as words because they cannot be transmitted by telegraph:

   a. ¢—should be written "cent" or "cents."
   b. @—should be written "at."
   c. °—should be written "degree" or "degrees."

9. In domestic service, most symbols, such as $, &, #, and /, can be transmitted and are counted and charged at the rate of one word for each five figures (including symbols) and letters.

10. The percent sign (%) is transmitted as o/o and counts as three characters.

11. Each group of figures or mixed figures and letters is counted as one word for each five characters. With figures the decimal point, the comma, quotation marks, and the dash are considered to be marks of punctuation and therefore are not counted.

> KKM/MM (2 words)
> KMM-6542 (2 words)
> X80946534 (2 words—9 characters)
> A60-RX43M (2 words)
> 6th (one word)

12. Each word in the names of cities, states, and countries is counted; as New Mexico (2 words), New York City (3 words).

Conducting and Reporting Business Meetings

Those who work in offices are frequently called upon to conduct or to participate in business meetings. Although some business meetings are conducted formally according to strict rules of order, most business meetings are conducted informally. A written report (similar to the minutes of an organization) is usually kept to record any business meeting—formal or informal.

18-1. Conducting a Formal Business Meeting

1. No meeting should be held unless there is a quorum present. Usually a quorum represents more than one half of the membership, but the organization may fix the quorum at any number.

2. A meeting should be started at the scheduled time and should have a definite purpose.

3. Certain expressions have become fixed or traditional in parliamentary procedure, such as the presiding officer's opening remark, "The meeting will please come to order."

4. Unless some other form of procedure has been prescribed, the following order may be used:

   a. Roll call
   b. Reading of the minutes of the previous meeting
   c. Approval of the minutes
   d. Committee reports
   e. Unfinished or old business
   f. New business
   g. Adjournment

5. During the business meeting, any member who wishes to speak should rise and address the presiding officer as "Mr. Chairman," "Mr. President," "Madam President," or the like.

6. The officer will then recognize the individual by speaking his name or by giving a nod of recognition.

7. The member then states his business. If he desires to make a motion, he should say, "I move that . . . ."

8. A second is necessary to make the motion valid. If it is not forthcoming voluntarily, the chairman will ask, "Is there a second to this motion?" To second the motion, a member needs no

MINUTES OF THE MEETING

OF THE

OFFICE MANAGEMENT ASSOCIATION

    The regular monthly meeting of the Office Management Associa-
tion was held at the Hotel Carter on Monday evening, July 8, 19--.
At 8 p.m. Mr. John Downs, the President, called the meeting to
order with a word of welcome to the new members and guests. Since
a number of those present were attending this meeting for the first
time, Mr. Downs briefly outlined the history and purpose of the
organization.

    Roll call was taken in the usual manner. There were 49 mem-
bers and 3 guests present; 6 members were absent.

    The minutes of the previous meeting were read and approved.

    The President called for the reports of the Treasurer, of
the Corresponding Secretary, and of the standing committees.

    The Treasurer's report, which was accepted as read, was as
follows:

Balance on Hand, June 10, 19--..	$1,321.17
Receipts.....................	47.99
Gross Assets..............	$1,369.16
Disbursements...............	84.16
Balance on Hand, July 8, 19--...	$1,285.00

    The Corresponding Secretary, Miss Mary Hall, reported that
only a few requests had been received for the pamphlets published
by the Association on subjects discussed at the convention in May.

Committee Reports

    Education Committee. Miss Helen Mason, Chairman, reported
that her committee was making plans for an open meeting in November to which all interested in office supervision will be invited.

    Membership Committee. Mr. Arthur Wall announced that his
committee is working on a new membership campaign.

    Publicity Committee. Mr. Richard Kelly, Chairman, reported
that the local newspapers and a number of magazines devoted to

18

18-a. Minutes of a Meeting (First Page)

2

office management carried interesting articles about the effective work of our organization.

Program Committee. No report.

Old Business

The President urged a display of greater interest in the contest for developing a symbolic emblem for the Association. He announced that only a few had participated and that the Executive Committee had decided to postpone the closing date until August.

Mr. Lawrence Smith, Chairman of the Program Committee, announced that the trip planned to the Bronson Box Company would be postponed to an indefinite date in the fall. Vacation plans necessitated the cancellation of many reservations.

New Business

Mr. James Fuerst called the attention of the members to the many books now available on office management and said that upon request he would be glad to give each member a list of the most recent publications.

A discussion was held on the suspension of the August meeting. Differences of opinion were expressed. Mr. Walter Harring made a motion that the meeting be suspended in August. The motion was seconded and carried. Accordingly Mr. Downs announced that the next meeting date of the Association would be the second Monday in September. He extended wishes for a happy summer and urged a complete membership attendance at the first fall meeting.

Adjournment

There being no further business, the meeting was adjourned at 9:30 p.m.

Respectfully submitted

Joanne Winterick
Joanne Winterick
Recording Secretary

18-a. Minutes of a Meeting (Second Page)

recognition from the chairman. The member simply says, "I second the motion."

9. The chairman continues, "It has been moved and seconded that . . . . Is there any discussion?"

10. At the close of the discussion, the chairman asks, "Are you ready for the question?"

11. When a member wishes to close the discussion, he merely calls "Question." The effect of "Question" in either case is to call for a vote on the motion.

12. The chairman then repeats the motion and says, "All those in favor signify by raising the right hand (saying 'Aye,' or rising); all opposed signify by raising the right hand (saying 'No,' or rising)."

13. A procedure for disposing of a motion without voting on it is to "lay it on the table" or to "call for an adjournment."

14. A pending motion must be disposed of before a second motion may be introduced. Should an amendment be made to a motion, the amendment must be voted on before the main motion may be considered.

15. When all business has been disposed of or when a time limit has been reached, the chairman may say, "A motion for adjournment is in order," or "Is there a motion for adjournment?" This motion may also come directly from a member. In either case the motion must have a second and must receive a majority vote.

18-2. Reporting a Formal Business Meeting

1. The minutes should set forth the kind of meeting (regular or special), the place, the date, the time, and the purpose. If possible, the stenographer should refer to a previous record of minutes to ascertain the form.

2. The record must contain both the positive and the negative opinions that were expressed in the discussion.

3. Single spacing or double spacing may be used in typing the report. A two-inch top margin should be allowed on the first page, similar to the style used in manuscript writing.

4. The illustration on pages 162 and 163 may be used as a model report.

18-3. Conducting an Informal Business Meeting

1. Usually each informal business meeting is called for a specific purpose. Each meeting is attended by those who have an interest or a voice in the matter at hand. As the meeting progresses, additional people may be called in as a need for them develops.

2. The person who calls the meeting has an informal agenda in mind; he steers the dialogue informally to keep the participants on the

SUMMARY OF SALES STAFF MEETING

```
        TO:  John McGreal, President
      FROM:  Claude Hummingbird, Sales Manager
      DATE:  October 7, 19--
   SUBJECT:  Meeting of the Sales Staff, October 5, 19--
ATTENDANCE:  Messrs. Elmer, Grismere, Krygowski, Hummingbird
```

I. The following changes in sales territories are recommended:

    A. The western counties of Ohio which are contiguous to the Indiana state line be removed from Territory 5 and added to Territory 4.

    B. The metropolitan St. Paul area be removed from Territory 4 and added to Territory 6.

II. It is recommended that all other changes in territory pending at this time be tabled until the annual sales report is published in January.

III. It is recommended that the annual sales report be published in greater detail. The report should include all the data presently reported, plus the following:

    A. Classification of Customers
        1. Wholesale
        2. Retail
        3. Industrial
    B. Type of Product
        1. Paint, varnish, lacquer
        2. Solvent
        3. Others

18-b. Report of an Informal Business Meeting in Memorandum Form

subject. The meeting is conducted in conversational mode rather than according to specific rules of order.

3. Ideas are expressed freely; each participant judges the appropriateness and timing of his comments.

4. Most informal business meetings are for the purpose of communicating ideas rather than voting to reach decisions. The results usually take the form of recommendations rather than resolutions.

18-4. Reporting an Informal Business Meeting

1. The informal meeting is usually reported in a brief, pithy summary.
2. The report summarizes results; it does not describe the proceedings.
3. Considerable latitude in style is permissible.

Legal Documents

This unit presents a few of the practices followed in most law offices. Standardized legal forms, which vary from state to state, are available at stationers. These forms require the specific and pertinent information to be typed in appropriate blank spaces. Accuracy and painstaking care are required in the typing of legal forms. No erasures or changes in sums of money, dates, or names are permitted on legal documents.

19-1. Techniques for Typing Legal Documents

1. Use paper 8½ by 13 or 14 inches with double vertical rules at the left and a single vertical rule at the right. Set the stop for the left margin so that the typewritten work will be started 1 or 2 spaces to the right of the double ruling. Adjust the stop for the right margin so that the longest lines will end 1 or 2 spaces to the left of the single ruling.

2. If ruled paper is not available, set the margin stops for a left margin of 1½ inches and a right margin of ½ inch.

3. Unless otherwise instructed, make at least one carbon copy.

4. Use only one side of the paper.

5. Date all legal papers by either spelling out the date or writing it in figures.

> . . . this seventeenth day of December, nineteen hundred sixty-nine, . . .
> . . . this 17th day of December, 1969, . . .

6. Indent paragraphs 10 spaces.

7. Double-space unless other instructions are given.

8. Center the heading approximately 2 inches from the top of the form.

9. Triple-space between the heading and the first line.

10. Begin the second and succeeding pages 2 inches from the top.

11. Allow at least an inch margin at the bottom of the page. This margin should be uniform on all pages.

12. Do not number the first page, except on a will. Center all other page numbers between the marginal rulings ½ inch from the bottom of the page. Do not use periods after the numbers. Instead, use a hyphen before and a hyphen after, as follows:

-2-

13. Capitalize according to the style of the office.

19

14. Omit a title before the name of a person.

Ralph A. Brown, the party of the first part

not

Mr. Ralph A. Brown, the party of the first part

15. Express sums of money in words and figures.

One Thousand Two Hundred Twenty-five (1,225) dollars

or

One Thousand Two Hundred Twenty-five Dollars ($1,225)

16. Type copies of legal documents verbatim, including the errors and corrections. Some typists prefer to underscore the uncorrected errors to show that they appeared in the original copy.

19-2. Acceptable Methods of Making Corrections

1. Corrections may be recorded on a special list that is then attached to the original document.

2. Errors made in sums of money, dates, or names may be X'd out. The correct form is typed immediately following.

3. Errors not involving sums of money, dates, or names may be erased and corrected on the original and carbon copies.

19-3. Boxings and Backing Sheets

1. The boxings or headings used in legal documents vary according to the many firms engaged in legal work. States differ, too, in the style of caption used; but the information contained in these boxings generally identifies the locality of the court, gives the names of the parties concerned, and indicates the nature of the proceedings.

2. Legal papers and documents are generally bound with backing sheets on which endorsements or "briefs" showing the contents are made. Backing sheets, made of heavier stock than the stationery used for the legal documents, measure about 1 inch wide and 1½ inches longer than the document. The following steps should be followed when preparing a backing sheet:

    a. Fold the upper edge of the backing sheet down 1 inch and crease.

    b. Bring the lower edge up to this crease and fold.

    c. Bring the second crease up to the crease made in Step *a* and fold.

    d. Unfold this last crease and insert the sheet in the typewriter so that the fold made in Step *b* will be at the right of the platen.

    e. Type the endorsement.

    f. Insert the document under the inch fold at the top of the backing sheet and staple.

    g. Refold according to the original creases.

19

LAST WILL AND TESTAMENT
OF
JOHN A. ADAMS
Norwood, Ohio
May 10, 19--

Maddon & Wallace
Attorneys-at-Law
4106 Montgomery Road
Norwood, Ohio 45212

19-a. Endorsement

LAST WILL AND TESTAMENT OF JOHN A. ADAMS

I, JOHN A. ADAMS, of the City of Norwood, County of Hamilton, Ohio, being of sound and disposing mind and memory, do make, publish, and declare the following as and for my Last Will and Testament, hereby revoking all former wills, devises, and bequests by me at any time made:

FIRST: I direct my executors hereinafter named to pay my just debts, funeral expenses, and . . . .

SECOND: I give and bequeath the property which

FIFTH: I nominate and appoint . . . as executors of this my Last Will and Testament.

IN WITNESS WHEREOF, I have hereunto set my hand and seal at Norwood, Ohio, this tenth day of May, 19--.

_____(L.S.)

The foregoing instrument was on the date thereof signed, sealed, published, and declared by the said JOHN A. ADAMS as and for his Last Will and Testament, in the presence of us, and each of us, who, at his request, in his presence, and in the presence of each other have hereunto set our names as attesting witnesses.
We further certify that at the time of such signing the said JOHN A. ADAMS was of sound and disposing mind and memory and under no restraint.

_____ residing at _____

_____ residing at _____

19-b. A Sample Will Typed on Unruled Paper

```
STATE OF MICHIGAN    )
                     :
County of Menominee )

           On the twentieth day of July, 19--, before me, a
Notary Public, personally appeared CHARLES C. CONWAY, to me
known to be the plaintiff in the above action. . . .

           WITNESS my hand and official seal.


                            _____
                                 Notary Public
```

19-c. A Form of Acknowledgment

19-4. Abbreviations for Legal Terms

administrator	adm.
administratrix	admx.
Answer	Ans.
attorney	atty.
Bill of Particulars	B/P
et alibi (and elsewhere)	et al.
et alii, et aliae (and others)	et al.
et uxor (and wife)	et ux.
executor	exr.
executrix	exrx.
folio	f. *or* fol.
habeas corpus	hab. corp.
Jury Demand	J/D
locus sigilli (place of the seal)	L.S.
Notary Public	N.P.
Note of Issue	N/I
Notice of Appearance	N/A
Notice of Trial	N/T
Notice to Produce	N/P
Power of Attorney	P/A
Question	Q. *or* Ques.
regarding	re
Retainer Agreement	R/A
scilicet (to wit *or* namely)	ss. *or* SS.
versus (against)	vs. *or* v.

Manuscripts and Outlines

Typing of business reports, manuscripts, and articles for publication may be part of any typist's work. When such an assignment is given, no change should be made in the text of the report or manuscript without the consent of the author. The typist, however, should be sufficiently alert and competent to detect errors and to suggest revisions.

20-1. Author's Instructions

1. When the typing of a manuscript is assigned, the typist should ask for specific instructions about the following:

    a. The number of copies.
    b. The title page.
    c. The table of contents.
    d. Illustrations.
    e. The bibliography.
    f. Type of binding, if any.
    g. Any items which appear questionable as the copy is scanned quickly.

2. The typist should not waste time by reading *long* manuscripts in their entirety. She should read for correctness as she types each page. If the copy must be clarified, she should lay the page in question aside and continue typing subsequent pages if the paging arrangement permits.

20-2. Checklist of Materials

1. An ample supply of plain paper of good quality and 8½ by 11 inches in size. (Rag content of 50 percent or more is recommended.)

2. Carbon paper.

3. A typing eraser for correcting errors on the original typewritten copy.

4. A soft (pencil type) eraser for correcting errors on carbon copies.

5. A card (3 x 5, 4 x 6, etc.) to protect the carbon copies from smudging when errors are erased.

20-3. Typing of the Text (Body)

1. Plan the margins. (See the illustration on page 177.)

   a. If the manuscript is to be submitted unbound or stapled at the upper left corner:

      (1) Leave left, right, and bottom margins of 1 inch.
      (2) Leave a top margin of 1½ or 2 inches on the first page.
      (3) Leave a top margin of 1 inch on all pages after the first.

   b. If the manuscript is to be bound at the top:

      (1) Leave left, right, and bottom margins of 1 inch.
      (2) Leave a top margin of 2 or 2½ inches on the first page.
      (3) Leave a top margin of 1½ inches (type on Line 10) on all pages after the first.

   c. If the manuscript is to bound along the left edge:

      (1) Leave a 1½-inch margin at the left side of each page.
      (2) Leave bottom and right margins of 1 inch on all pages.
      (3) Leave a top margin of 1½ or 2 inches on the first page.
      (4) Leave a top margin of 1 inch (type on Line 7) on all pages after the first.

2. Type the headings in the following manner.

   a. Center the main title in solid capitals on the appropriate line. Two blank lines (space 3 times) should follow the main heading.

      Note: If the manuscript is to be bound at the left (with a 1½-inch left margin), center the headings on the writing line—not across the page.

   b. If the main title is followed by a centered subheading, follow these steps:

      (1) Type the main title as indicated above.
      (2) Double-space.
      (3) Type the subheading, capitalizing the first letter of each important word.
      (4) Triple-space.
      (5) Type the first line of the text.

   c. If sectional side headings are used, type them on separate lines flush with the left margin with a triple space before them and a double space after them.

3. Follow these conventions within the body.

   a. Begin a report or article 3 line spaces below the title. When a title page is used, begin the manuscript proper on a new page.
   b. Indent the paragraphs 5, 7, or 10 spaces; use double spacing.
   c. Single-space quotations of 4 or more lines and indent them 5 spaces from both the right and the left margins. Double-space quotations that are less than 4 lines in length.

20

d. Use [sic] in quoted material, the construction of which is or appears to be faulty. To illustrate:

> She never went to school, for she was born in the forest, at least more than two or three months, [sic] but she was the best-read member of our family.

e. Underscore all expressions that should appear in *italics*:

(1) Titles of books, magazines, music, newspapers, and works of art.

(2) For words not naturalized. (Such words may also be enclosed in quotation marks. See Rule 8-42: 1, page 81.)

(3) Any word under discussion or requiring emphasis.

(4) Expressions such as *To be continued, Continued, Concluded on page 48,* etc.

f. Indicate footnotes with superior figures, asterisks, or other symbols.

g. Attach charts, graphs, or other illustrative materials.

h. If desired, indicate the completion of a short manuscript by centering "###" 3 line spaces below the last line. On longer manuscripts, use the word "Finis."

i. Proofread your work carefully.

4. Insert footnotes.

a. Type footnotes to give credit for actual words quoted or ideas that supplement the author's opinions. Use footnotes also to call attention to other parts of the report or to explain technical terms in the text.

b. Call attention to each footnote by placing a superior number or symbol (corresponding to the one identifying the footnote) at the right of the appropriate word or sentence. (In numbered tabulations, the symbol may appear at the left of the item.)

c. Type a line 1½ inches long below the last line of the text to separate the footnotes from the text. Begin the line at the left margin and at least a double space below the last line of the text. (See Illustration 20-d on page 177.)

d. Use either superior numbers (coefficients) or symbols to identify footnotes.

> **Note:** The symbols may be * (asterisk), † (dagger), ‡ (double dagger), § (section), // (parallel), and ¶ (paragraph). For additional symbols, double and triple the sequence.

e. Single-space footnotes; double-space between footnotes.

f. Type the footnotes to which the reference figures or symbols refer on the same page on which those reference figures or symbols occur in the text.

g. Include in footnotes the following items:

(1) The author's name should be typed in normal order; it should be followed by the title of the work typed in italics.[1]

(2) The publication information should state the edition, the place of publication, the name of the publisher, and the date of publication. These items are enclosed in parentheses.[2]

(3) The title of a magazine article is enclosed in quotation marks; the name of the periodical is italicized.[3]

(4) Volume and page numbers are given when available. Roman numerals are used for volumes; Arabic numerals, for pages.

(5) The abbreviation *Ibid.* is used when reference is made to the same work cited in the footnote immediately preceding.[4]

(6) When reference is made to a different page in a work already cited but separated by intervening footnotes, the author's last name, followed by *op. cit.*, and the page number are used. This abbreviation should be used only when but one work of the particular author has been cited.[5]

(7) When reference is made to the same page of a work already cited but not immediately preceding, the abbreviation *loc. cit.* is used after the author's name.[6]

h. Refer to the footnotes shown at the bottom of this page as illustrations of the points just given.

i. Allow space of ½ inch for the average footnote. Some typists make a light warning pencil mark to remind them to allow for footnotes. The stopping point must be raised about ½ inch each time an additional footnote is indicated in the text.

j. You may prefer (instead of marking the stopping point with a pencil) to use a backing sheet marked off in increments of ½ inch. To use the backing sheet, begin the footnote section of the page when the number of footnotes indexed in the text equals the number on the backing sheet scale. Use the *line of writing* as the index point on the backing sheet scale.

---

[1] Francis Keppel, *The Necessary Revolution in American Education* (New York: Harper and Row, 1966), pp. 43-57.

[2] John A. Nietz, *The Evolution of American Secondary School Textbooks* (Rutland, Vermont: Charles E. Tuttle Co., 1966), p. 22.

[3] Shirley Angrist, "Leisure and the Educated Woman," *AAUW Journal* (October, 1966), p. 10.

[4] *Ibid.*, p. 11.

[5] Keppel, *op. cit.*, pp. 109-116.

[6] Nietz, *loc. cit.*

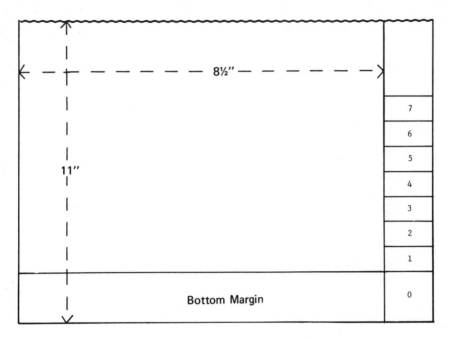

20-a. Backing Sheet for Manuscript Typing

20-4. Paging the Manuscript

1. Use Arabic numerals for all page numbers. If a manuscript requires only one page, no page number is required.
2. For a manuscript that is bound across the top, center the page number about ½ inch from the bottom of the sheet.
3. For a manuscript bound at the left, stapled in the upper left corner, or unbound, place the page number on the fourth line from the top of the page and align it with the right margin.
4. If desired, identify the second and following pages of an unbound manuscript by placing the title flush with the left margin on the same line as the page number.

20-5. Typing the Bibliography

1. Place the bibliography, in which the author identifies the sources of material for the manuscript or provides reference matter, either at the end of every chapter or at the close of the manuscript. (See the illustration of a bibliography on page 177.)
2. Include the following information:
   a. Name of each author. If a reference has only one author, the name of the author is transposed so that the surname is given first. If a reference has two or more authors, the name of only the first author is transposed; the names of the other authors

TABLE OF CONTENTS

20-c. Table of Contents

THE VALUE OF DIALOGUE IN MANAGEMENT

Claude Hummingbird
Eastern Business School

January 24, 19--

20-b. Title Page

BIBLIOGRAPHY

Anshen, Melvin, and George L. Bach. Management and Corporations, 1985. New York: McGraw-Hill Book Co., Inc., 1961.

Beaumont, Richard A., and Roy B. Helfgott. Management, Automation, and People. New York: Industrial Relations Counselors, 1964.

Howe, Reuel L. The Miracle of Dialogue. New York: The Seabury Press, 1963.

Marting, Elizabeth, and Dorothy Macdonald. Management and Its People. New York: American Management Association, 1965.

Richards, Max, and Paul S. Greenlaw. Management Decision Making. Richard D. Irwin, Inc., 1966.

20-e. Bibliography

THE VALUE OF DIALOGUE IN MANAGEMENT

Management is just beginning to weigh the relative values of unilateral control on the one hand and internal dialogue on the other.[1] The traditional line-and-staff organization may be on the road to extinction. It is presently difficult to determine the power or the speed of the movement, but some convincing evidence of its direction is accumulating.[2] Mature leaders, who have reached their various pinnacles of success, and noncompeting observers alike are concerned about the tendency of the chain-of-command organization to dwarf its men: to grind them down to the point that the organization is robbed of their commitment, their drive, and their involvement.

From the dawn of civilization men, in their quest for power, have sought control of nature, wealth, and other men. Historically, society has favored pyramidal structure. (Perhaps it would be more accurate to say that societies have been forced, persuaded, or convinced through superstition by a powerful minority to accept the pyramidal form of organization.) From the days of divine right and serfdom, power, centered at the apex, has been exercised through immediate lieutenants. These lieutenants control a larger number of subordinates, who in turn control an even larger number of

[1] Reuel L. Howe, The Miracle of Dialogue (New York: The Seabury Press, 1963), p. 27.

[2] Max Richards and Paul S. Greenlaw, Management Decision Making (Homewood, Illinois: Richard D. Irwin, 1966), p. 44.

20-d. First Page of a Manuscript

20-f. Rough Draft Showing the Use of Proofreader's Marks

2

people of lesser rank, so the nation, tribe, or business firm is
organized to execute the orders of the ruler, chief, or manager.

Totalitarianism: Result of the Pyramidal Form of organization

Most corporate organizational charts are designed in the
pattern of the old pyramidal model. Line and staff relationships
are clearly delineated; the chain of command is firmly established.
If employees are made to feel that the organization chart is the
blueprint from which the firm was constructed, and that the firm
is some sort of mechanical device that functions only according to the
specifications of the designer, they cannot contribute their best
efforts.

Line relationships tend to become chains of command and one-
way avenues of communication that stifle the initiative of those
who are too far from the top to be heard. Each echelon of management tends to screen out communication from below. Top management,
having isolated itself from those below, may attempt to solve the
problem with incentive programs, suggestion boxes, and advisory
committees. If programs such as these are operated in a climate
of good internal communications, they can function well. If they
are operated only as a meaningless gesture, the hypocrisy that
results further insulates top management. Recognizing the failure
to achieve satisfactory results, management may resort to more
efficiency studies, further clarification of the organizational
chart, and even more rigidity. A kind of industrial totalitarianism arises that ignores the value of dialogue and binds the firm
in bureaucratic chains of command.

20-g. Corrected Copy of Rough Draft Shown at the Left

2

people of lesser rank, so the nation, tribe, or business firm is
organized to execute the orders of the ruler, chief, or manager.

Totalitarianism: Result of the Pyramidal Form of Organization

Most corporate organizational charts are designed in the
pattern of the old pyramidal model. Line and staff relationships
are clearly delineated; the chain of command is firmly established.
If employees are made to feel that the organizational chart is the
blueprint from which the firm was constructed, and that the firm
is some sort of mechanical device that functions only according
to the specifications of the designer, they cannot contribute their
best efforts.

Line relationships tend to become chains of command and one-
way avenues of communication that stifle the initiative of those
who are too far from the top to be heard. Each echelon of management tends to screen out communication from below. Top management,
having isolated itself from those below, may attempt to solve the
problem with incentive programs, suggestion boxes, and advisory
committees. If programs such as these are operated in a climate
of good internal communications, they can function well. If they
are operated only as a meaningless gesture, the hypocrisy that
results further insulates top management. Recognizing the failure
to achieve satisfactory results, management may resort to more
efficiency studies, "further clarification" of the organizational
chart, and even more rigidity. A kind of industrial totalitarianism arises that ignores the value of dialogue and binds the firm
in bureaucratic chains of command.

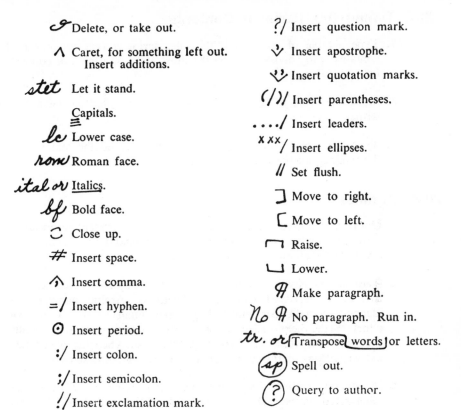

ℰ Delete, or take out.	?/ Insert question mark.
∧ Caret, for something left out. Insert additions.	⋎ Insert apostrophe.
stet Let it stand.	⋎⋎ Insert quotation marks.
Capitals.	(/)/ Insert parentheses.
lc Lower case.	..../ Insert leaders.
rom Roman face.	x xx/ Insert ellipses.
ital or Italics.	// Set flush.
bf Bold face.	] Move to right.
⌒ Close up.	[Move to left.
# Insert space.	⌐ Raise.
⌃ Insert comma.	⌄ Lower.
=/ Insert hyphen.	¶ Make paragraph.
⊙ Insert period.	*No* ¶ No paragraph. Run in.
:/ Insert colon.	*tr. or* Transpose words or letters.
;/ Insert semicolon.	*sp* Spell out.
!/ Insert exclamation mark.	(?) Query to author.

20-h. Proofreader's Marks

are given in normal order. The transposition of the name of the only author or of the first of several authors aids in the alphabetic arrangement of the entries.

b. Title of the work in italics.
   (Magazine articles are enclosed in quotation marks, and the name of the publication is italicized.)

c. Place of publication, name of the publisher, and date of publication.

3. Arrange the references in alphabetic order according to surnames.

20-6. Typing the Title Page

1. On the title page show the title of the manuscript, the name of the author, and the date. (See the illustration of a title page on page 176.)

2. Include additional information if desired. The arrangement should be appropriate to the type of report or article.

20-7. Typing the Table of Contents

1. Type a table of contents if the manuscript is very long or if it contains many divisions. (See the illustration of a table of contents on page 176.)

2. Make the table of contents as long or as detailed as the author wishes.

3. Type the table of contents after you have typed the text so that the paging can be ascertained easily.

20-8. Outlines

1. Outlines are often used in business writing to present information in a form that is concise and easy to understand or to summarize information about a particular subject.

2. Outlines use Roman numerals to identify major divisions, capital letters to identify first-order subheadings, Arabic numerals to identify second-order subheadings, and small letters to identify items in the next order. If still other subdivisions are needed, numbers and letters in parentheses are used. (See the illustration at the bottom of this page for an outline of these steps.)

3. In general, outlines are typed according to either of the styles illustrated on pages 181 and 182. The difference between the two styles is in the capitalization. Both styles are widely used.

```
I.  ------------------
    A. ------------------
    B. ------------------
       1. ------------------
       2. ------------------
       3. ------------------
          a. ------------------
          b. ------------------
             (1) ------------------
             (2) ------------------
                 (a) ------------------
                 (b) ------------------
                 (c) ------------------

II. ------------------
    A. ------------------
    B. ------------------
       1. ------------------
       2. ------------------
```

**20-i. Outline Form Showing Numbers and Letters
Designating Parts of an Outline**

INVESTMENTS

I. The securities markets

    A. Limited income securities
    B. Common stocks
       1. Growth factors
       2. Investment strategies
       3. Valuation Theories

II. Institutional securities

    A. Banking and savings institutions
       1. Commercial banks
          a. Savings function
          b. Monetary function
       2. Mutual savings banks
       3. Savings and loan associations
    B. Insurance companies, pension funds,
       and nonprofit organizations

20-j. A Widely Used Form of Outline

INVESTMENTS

I. THE SECURITIES MARKETS

    A. Limited Income Securities
    B. Common Stocks
        1. Growth factors
        2. Investment strategies
        3. Valuation theories

II. INSTITUTIONAL SECURITIES

    A. Banking and Savings Institutions
        1. Commercial banks
            a. Savings function
            b. Monetary function
        2. Mutual savings banks
        3. Savings and loan associations
    B. Insurance Companies, Pension Funds, and Nonprofit Organizations

20-k. A Second Widely Used Form of Outline

Sources of Information

Few office libraries are sufficiently exhaustive to meet the unusual questions that are apt to arise. For that reason the facilities of public and private libraries may be used to supplement the reference books available in the office. Although the following list is not comprehensive, it attempts to suggest sources of information and to give a skeleton idea of their particular purposes.

21-1. Sources of Information—Books

1. Dictionary—authorized unabridged or abridged for definitions, pronunciations, abbreviations, foreign phrases, biographical listings, and gazeteer.

2. Book of synonyms and antonyms—
   a. *Roget's International Thesaurus of English Words and Phrases*
   b. *Webster's Dictionary of Synonyms*

3. Stylebooks of English—See the listings in Section 21-4 of this unit.

4. Encyclopedia—a source of general information treating all kinds of subjects, arranged alphabetically.

5. Directories—
   a. Telephone directories—alphabetic and classified
   b. City directories
   c. Other directories—professional and trade

6. Other publications—
   a. Almanacs—*World Almanac*—statistical and historical information on government, finance, labor, trade, commerce, astronomical data.
   b. Atlas—Rand, McNally & Co.'s *Commercial Atlas and Marketing Guide.*
   c. Bullinger's *Postal and Shippers Guide for the United States, Canada, and Newfoundland.*
   d. *Official Hotel Red Book and Directory.*
   e. Trade Journals.
   f. *The Postal Manual.*
   g. *Who's Who*—an English publication of prominent people from any country.
   h. *Who's Who in America*—short biographies of living Americans.

21-2. Other Sources of Information

1. Local information service bureaus—Better Business Bureau, Chamber of Commerce, etc.

2. Newspaper service bureaus.

3. Credit agencies—Dun & Bradstreet, Inc., Moody, etc.

4. United States Government, Department of Interior, or U.S. Government Printing Office, Washington, D.C.   20402.

5. Public library.

    a. *Reader's Guide to Periodical Literature*—lists of magazine articles by author and subject.

    b. Card catalog—alphabetic index by name, author, and subject of all classified material.

21-3. The Dewey Decimal System of Cataloging

1. Most libraries use the Dewey Decimal System of cataloging and arrange their books on the shelves according to this numeric classification.

2. Familiarity with the general scheme of numbering shown below will enable an individual to locate independently the book sections desired.

      000—General
      100—Philosophy
      200—Religion
    *300—Social Science
      400—Language
      500—Science and Mathematics
    *600—Applied Sciences and Industries
      700—Fine Arts and Recreation
      800—Literature
      900—History, Travel, and Biography

21-4. Bibliography

Agnew, Peter L., James R. Meehan, and Mary Ellen Oliverio. *Secretarial Office Practice,* 7th ed. Cincinnati: South-Western Publishing Co., 1966.

Agnew, Peter L., James R. Meehan, and William R. Pasework. *Clerical Office Practice,* 4th ed. Cincinnati: South-Western Publishing Co., 1967.

Aurner, Robert Ray, and Paul S. Burtness. *Effective English for Business Communication,* 6th ed. Cincinnati: South-Western Publishing Co., 1970.

Aurner, Robert Ray, and Morris P. Wolf. *Effective Communication in Business,* 5th ed. Cincinnati: South-Western Publishing Co., 1967.

Becker, Esther R. *Success and Satisfaction in Your Office Job.* New York: Harper & Brothers, 1954.

* These sections contain most of the books on business problems.

21

Brown, Leland. *Communicating Facts and Ideas in Business.* New York: Prentice-Hall, Inc., 1961.

Buckley, Earle A. *How to Write Better Business Letters,* 4th ed. New York: McGraw-Hill Book Co., Inc., 1957.

Butterfield, W. H. *Common Sense in Letter Writing.* New York: Prentice-Hall, Inc., 1963.

Delano, Margaret. *How to Be a Top Secretary.* Atlanta: Tupper & Love, 1954.

Doris, L., and Bessie May Miller. *Complete Secretary's Handbook.* New York: Prentice-Hall, Inc., 1960.

Frailey, L. E. *Handbook of Business Letters.* New York: Prentice-Hall, Inc., 1965.

Gorrell, R. M., and C. G. Laird. *Modern English Handbook.* New York: Prentice-Hall, Inc., 1963.

Hanna, J Marshall, Estelle L. Popham, and Esther K. Beamer. *Secretarial Procedures and Administration,* 5th ed. Cincinnati: South-Western Publishing Co., 1968.

Hutchinson, Lois I. *Standard Handbook for Secretaries,* 8th ed. New York: McGraw-Hill Book Co., Inc., 1969.

Johnson, H. Webster. *How to Use the Business Library,* 3d ed. Cincinnati: South-Western Publishing Co., 1964.

Keithley, Erwin M. *A Manual of Style for the Preparation of Papers and Reports.* Cincinnati: South-Western Publishing Co., 1959.

Keithley, Erwin M., and Margaret H. Thompson. *English for Modern Business.* Homewood, Illinois: Richard D. Irwin, Inc., 1966.

Laird, Donald A., and Eleanor C. *Practical Business Psychology,* 3d ed. New York: McGraw-Hill Book Co., Inc., 1961.

Lessenberry, D. D., S. J. Wanous, and C. H. Duncan. *College Typewriting,* 8th ed. Cincinnati: South-Western Publishing Co., 1969.

MacGibbon, Elizabeth G. *Fitting Yourself for Business.* New York: McGraw-Hill Book Co., Inc., 1961.

A Manual of Style, 12th ed. Chicago: The University of Chicago Press, 1969.

Marra, W. J. *Streamlined Letters.* St. Louis: Retail Credit Association, 1955.

Menning, J. H., and C. W. Wilkinson. *Communicating Through Letters and Reports,* 4th ed. Homewood, Illinois: Richard D. Irwin, Inc., 1967.

Miller, Bessie May. *The Legal Secretary's Complete Handbook.* New York: Prentice-Hall, Inc., 1953.

Newton, Roy, and Helen Green. *How to Improve Your Personality,* 3d ed. New York: McGraw-Hill Book Co., Inc., 1963.

O'Rourke, L. J. *Self-Aids in English Usage.* Lake Alfred, Florida: Psychological Institute, 1956.

Parkhurst, Charles C. *English for Business.* New York: Prentice-Hall, Inc., 1963.

Parkhurst, Charles C. *Business Communication for Better Human Relations.* New York: Prentice-Hall, Inc., 1966.

Pence, Raymond W. *A Grammar of Present-Day English.* New York: Macmillan Co., 1963.

Pendery, John, and Theodore Woodward. *General Office Practice for Colleges*, 5th ed. Cincinnati: South-Western Publishing Co., 1965.

Pendery, John A., and Theodore Woodward. *Secretarial Office Practice for Colleges*, 5th ed. Cincinnati: South-Western Publishing Co., 1965.

Place, Irene, and Charles B. Hicks. *College Secretarial Procedures*, 3d ed. New York: McGraw-Hill Book Co., Inc., 1964.

Place, Irene, and Madeline Strony. *The Road to Secretarial Success.* New York: McGraw-Hill Book Co., Inc., 1954.

Reigner, C. G. *College Secretarial Practice*. Chicago: The H. M. Rowe Co., Inc., 1960.

Riebel, J. P. *How to Write Successful Business Letters in 15 Days.* New York: Prentice-Hall, Inc., 1955.

Robertson, Horace O., and Vernal Carmichael. *Business Letter English.* New York: McGraw-Hill Book Co., Inc., 1957.

Rosenthal, Irving, and H. W. Rudman. *Business Letter Writing Made Simple.* Garden City, New York: Doubleday & Co., Inc., 1968.

Schwartz, Robert J. *The Complete Dictionary of Abbreviations.* New York: Thomas Y. Crowell Co., 1959.

Shaw, Harry, and Richard H. Dodge. *The Shorter Handbook of College Composition.* New York: Harper and Row, 1965.

Shurter, Robert L., and J. Peter Williamson. *Written Communication in Business*, 2d ed. New York: McGraw-Hill Book Co., Inc., 1964.

Silverthorn, J. E., and Devern J. Perry. *Word Division Manual*, 2d ed. Cincinnati: South-Western Publishing Co., 1970.

Smart, Walter K., Louis W. McKelvey, and Richard C. Gerfen. *Business Letters.* New York: Harper & Row, 1957.

Style Manual, Rev. ed. Washington, D.C.: U.S. Government Printing Office, 1967.

Taintor, Sarah A., and Kate M. Monro. *The Secretary's Handbook*, 9th ed. New York: Macmillan Co., 1969.

Thomas, Robert C., James M. Ethridge, and Frederick G. Ruffner, Jr. *Acronyms and Initialisms Dictionary*, 2d ed. Detroit: Gale Research Co., 1965.

Wanous, S. J., and L. W. Erickson. *The Secretary's Book.* New York: The Ronald Press Co., 1952.

Index

In this index, the bold-faced numbers refer to pages of the text. The light-faced numbers within parentheses refer to unit breakdowns. To locate a reference quickly, turn to the desired page number and then locate the unit breakdown on that page. For example, in an indexing item such as "and/or, **69** (8-21:2),"

69 indicates the page number.

8-21 indicates the section number.

2 indicates the subdivision of the section number.

In a few entries, a letter is given at the end of the number in the parentheses. This letter indicates a lettered item under the subdivision of the section.

CONTENTS

By matching up the guides at the edge of this page with the marks opposite them along the edge of the book, you can quickly turn to the unit containing the material you want.